CAESAR ENGLISH II

CLASSICAL EDUCATION EDITION
PART 2

Second Edition

Michael Clay Thompson
Myriam Borges Thompson
Thomas Milton Kemnitz

Royal Fireworks Press
Unionville, New York

Photo by Dr. Thomas Milton Kemnitz

LESSON XI · LATIN STEMS

stem	meaning	modern examples	Spanish
grat	pleasing	gratification, ingratiate, gratuitous	*gratificación*
curr	run	current, recur, incur	*incurrir*
trans	across	transfer, transfusion, transcendent	*transcendente*
migr	wander	migrate, migratory, transmigration	*transmigración*
rupt	break	abrupt, corrupt, disrupt	*abrupto*

GRAT means pleasing. *Gratification* is when you are pleased, to *ingratiate* yourself with someone means trying to please him or her, and a *gratuitous* assumption is unfounded; it is one that might please you, but it has no good reason or evidence, so it is pleasing but probably false.

CURR means run. A *current* runs in a stream; something *recurs* when it happens again, like a rerun; and to *incur* costs means to run into them.

TRANS means across. To *transfer* means to move things across from one place to another, a *transfusion* moves blood across from one person to another, and *transcendent* things are superior—they cross beyond anything previously done.

MIGR means wander. To *migrate* is to wander or move to a new place; *migratory* birds fly south for the winter, as though they were wandering through the skies; and the *transmigration* of souls is the idea that souls wander to a new being at death.

RUPT means break. An *abrupt* change is a sharp break in an event, a *corrupt* official has broken morals, and to *disrupt* an event is to break it up.

REVIEW STEMS FROM *CAESAR'S ENGLISH I*

stem	meaning	modern examples
spec	look	specter, specious, spectrum
pend	hang	pending, impending, depend
omni	all	omnipotent, omnivorous, omniscient
re	again	reiterate, regurgitate, revive
ex	out	exculpate, exorbitant, except

municant transfer patricide compete

sition maternity depopulate matricide

n comfort paternal vitamin transform

nport immigrate transcript patrilineal

rador incur patronize video transitive

mence matrimony invidious combine

ide company transcend commination

sm vital transmigrate abrupt commix

binative transfix retransmit compress

nend populous paternity transoceanic

nute ingratitude gratuitious patronize

e mand transect populace matrilocal

ze matrilineal composite mistranslate

atronage vide transmigrate ingratiate

lecommission transgression evidence

paternoster revitalize transcendental

video migrate expatriated matriarch

precognition congratulate transaction

epone grateful transcultural videlicet

alism migratory corruption prejudge

NONFICTION WORDS

Here are five important nonfiction words. You might not hear them often in daily conversation, but you will encounter them frequently in your future academic life. Each word is based on one of the stems in the lesson.

stem	word	definition
grat	**gratuitous**	uncalled for
curr	**concur**	to agree
trans	**transcend**	to go beyond limits
migr	**migratory**	moving seasonally
rupt	**disruption**	a disturbing interruption

GRATUITOUS is an adjective that means uncalled for, unfounded, or unmerited. In Thomas Hardy's 1886 novel *The Mayor of Casterbridge*, he wrote that "A gratuitous ordeal was in store for her in the matter of her handwriting." Henry David Thoreau used *gratuitous* in his 1854 *Walden* to say that we should care for our neighbor: "We should feed and clothe him gratuitously sometimes."

CONCUR is a verb that means to agree or sometimes to happen at the same time, to coincide. A noun form is *concurrence*. In Charles Dickens's *David Copperfield,* we read that "it could not be done without Mr. Mills's sanction and concurrence."

TRANSCEND is a verb that refers to going beyond something's range or limits. In *A Passage to India*, E.M. Forster described "the Lord of the Universe, who transcends human processes."

MIGRATORY is an adjective that refers literally to the seasonal moving of birds or other animals but metaphorically to human events. An example: His thoughts slowly migrated to his dreams of being a writer.

DISRUPTION is a noun that refers to an interruption that is disburbing. A clamorous spectator might cause a distruption in court procedings.

Write two good sentences for each word.

GRATUITOUS

CAESAR'S ANALOGIES: Find the most similar pairs.

TOADY : INGRATIATE ::
a. current : event
b. corrupt : crime
c. transfuse : blood
d. bird : migrate

TRANSFER : GOODS ::
a. hunger : gratify
b. corrupt : money
c. transfuse : blood
d. costs : incur

CAESAR'S ANTONYMS: Find the best opposite.

INCUR
a. avoid
b. recur
c. current
d. transfer

GRATUITOUS
a. transcendent
b. justified
c. corrupt
d. disrupted

CAESAR'S CONTEXT: Find the best word to complete the sentence.

Caesar believed that his military abilities were _____.
a. ambuscaded
b. current
c. transcendent
d. disrupted

The senators believed that Caesar's decision was merely _____.
a. recurring
b. omniscient
c. migratory
d. gratuitous

Barbarian uprisings _____ in Gaul throughout the decade.
a. recurred
b. transfused
c. transmigrated
d. reiterated

CAESAR'S CLASSIC WORDS CHALLENGE

If we want to get a feel for how words are used, we must see how great writers use words. In each case below, one of the choices was the word used by the author. For you, this is a word game. Your challenge is to guess which word the author used. This is not a test; it is a game because more than one word choice may work perfectly well. See if you can use your sensitivity and intuition to guess which word the author used. You may need a dictionary.

1. From Charles Dickens's *David Copperfield*

   This was entirely a _____ assumption.
   - a. recurrent
   - b. corrupt
   - c. gratuitous
   - d. transcendent

2. From James Hilton's *Lost Horizon*

   Shangri-La was interesting enough to _____ these attitudes.
   - a. disrupt
   - b. incur
   - c. transmigrate
   - d. transcend

3. From Joseph Conrad's *Lord Jim*

   He kept on trying to _____ himself with all.
   - a. ingratiate
   - b. transfer
   - c. disrupt
   - d. migrate

CAESAR'S MATHEMATICS

CLXXVIII introspective Romans made gratuitous criticisms of an idealistic politician. The criticisms caused a disruption in the streets, and centurions forced XLIX of the citizens to move on. Of the remainder, XXXVII citizens tried to transcend their former attitudes and concur with the idealistic politician, but the rest continued muttering and issuing mortifying remarks when they should have been affable. How many citizens continued to issue mortifying remarks?

CAESAR'S ESSAY

Academic writing observes certain standards of tone that other kinds of writing do not. Academic writing is calm, reserved, and formal. It does not use slang, first person, contractions, interjections, or other elements that would be appropriate in a short story or a personal letter. Academic writing is impersonal; it focuses on the knowledge concerning its topic. It is about truth, not feelings. It does not preach or scold the reader. It does not feature unsupported opinions, exclamation points, or appeals to the reader's emotions. It simply explains what the facts are and what conclusions may be drawn from them.

Read about the history of Constantinople, and write a short essay having something to do with that topic. As you read, pay attention to the scholarly, unemotional tone of academic writing, and try to use a clear, calm voice in your essay. Remember to use some of our advanced vocabulary.

TRANSCEND

CAESAR'S WORD SEARCH

In the puzzle, find the Latin-based English words that you see below. They might be vertical, horizontal, or diagonal. Always notice the stems that are in the words.

R	U	C	E	R	I	P	E	V	I	S	N	E	P	N
S	A	N	G	U	I	N	E	G	U	R	K	S	M	D
M	E	L	A	N	C	H	O	L	Y	H	D	A	M	Y
R	J	Y	F	I	T	R	O	M	I	I	S	G	E	R
E	T	A	D	I	C	U	L	E	S	A	P	R	G	O
I	C	O	N	C	U	R	Y	R	Z	G	F	A	A	T
Z	T	R	A	N	S	F	U	S	I	O	N	T	S	A
J	H	Z	B	D	I	P	R	O	T	X	E	U	I	R
Q	H	L	R	H	T	A	C	I	T	E	L	I	V	G
E	D	I	C	I	G	E	R	W	N	U	B	T	R	I
X	L	C	O	W	Q	P	E	T	P	Q	A	O	R	M
V	I	N	C	U	R	N	W	D	A	I	F	U	V	P
D	N	E	C	S	N	A	R	T	V	L	F	S	F	X
P	B	T	C	N	U	J	D	A	I	B	A	S	K	Y
A	M	P	R	U	D	N	S	N	D	O	W	Z	P	I

gratuitous	transfusion	affable	melancholy
concur	recur	sanguine	visage
transcend	incur	torpid	regicide
migratory	tacit	mortify	elucidate
disruption	adjunct	pensive	oblique

1. Which of these words has the nicest sound?
2. Which of these words might you use in a science essay?
3. Which two words are most similar in some interesting way?
4. Which word will you use most often? Why?
5. Which word has the clearest meaning?

CAESAR'S GRAMMAR · PHRASES

In Lessons I through V, we studied how vocabulary is used in the parts of speech. In Lessons VI through X, we studied the role vocabulary plays in parts of sentence. Now we will examine the part vocabulary plays in our phrases. A phrase is a group of words that acts as a single part of speech. In other words, it acts like one word, even though it is made of several words. We will study several kinds of phrases in this text; for more complete treatment of phrases, see *Grammar Voyage*, the grammar text for this level of the MCT curriculum.

Prepositional Phrases

We have seen many prepositional phrases in previous lessons. Prepositional phrases act like adjectives or adverbs, and they always begin with prepositions. If I say "the dog on the dock," the phrase *on the dock* acts as an adjective to modify the noun *dog*.

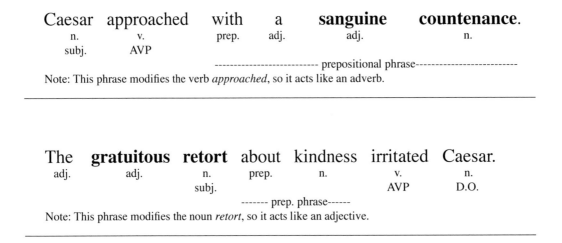

Caesar approached with a **sanguine** **countenance**.
n. v. prep. adj. adj. n.
subj. AVP
------------------------- prepositional phrase------------------------
Note: This phrase modifies the verb *approached*, so it acts like an adverb.

The **gratuitous** **retort** about kindness irritated Caesar.
adj. adj. n. prep. n. v. n.
subj. AVP D.O.
------- prep. phrase------
Note: This phrase modifies the noun *retort*, so it acts like an adjective.

Gerund Phrases as Subjects or Direct Objects

We know that some verbs, such as the progressive verbs, end in *-ing*. If I say "I am eating now," *am* and *eating* are both verbs. Sometimes, however, we use such verb forms in different ways.

A gerund is a verb form ending in *-ing* but used as a noun. We will look at gerund phrases that are used as the subjects or direct objects of sentences. In the sentence "Eating pizza is fun," *Eating pizza* is the gerund phrase used as the subject. Here is another:

Reiterating	the	**edict**		is	a	waste	of	time.
n.	adj.	n.		v.	adj.	n.	prep.	n.

----------------------subj.------------------   LVP   S.C.

------------------gerund phrase-----------   ---- prep. phrase----

Note: The entire gerund phrase acts as a noun and as the subject of the linking verb.

Introductory Participial Phrases

Unlike gerunds, which always end in *-ing*, a participle is any kind of verb form used as an adjective. An introductory participial phrase acts as an adjective to modify the subject of the sentence. In the sentence "Eating pizza, Mortimer remembered a story," the phrase *Eating pizza* acts as an adjective to modify the subject of the sentence, *Mortimer*. Introductory participial phrases come at the beginning of the sentence, they modify the subject, and they are set off by a comma.

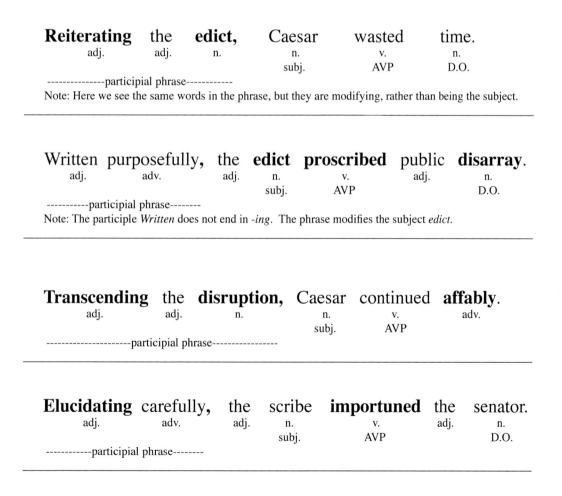

Reiterating	the	**edict,**	Caesar	wasted	time.
adj.	adj.	n.	n.	v.	n.
			subj.	AVP	D.O.

---------------participial phrase-----------

Note: Here we see the same words in the phrase, but they are modifying, rather than being the subject.

Written	purposefully,	the	**edict**	**proscribed**	public	**disarray.**
adj.	adv.	adj.	n.	v.	adj.	n.
			subj.	AVP		D.O.

-----------participial phrase--------

Note: The participle *Written* does not end in *-ing*. The phrase modifies the subject *edict*.

Transcending	the	**disruption,**	Caesar	continued	**affably.**
adj.	adj.	n.	n.	v.	adv.
			subj.	AVP	

--------------------participial phrase----------------

Elucidating	carefully,	the	scribe	**importuned**	the	senator.
adj.	adv.	adj.	n.	v.	adj.	n.
			subj.	AVP		D.O.

-----------participial phrase-------

CAESAR'S GRAMMAR · PHRASES

The first three sentences below are worked out for you. See if you can solve the next four, identifying the parts of speech, parts of sentence, and phrases for each sentence. Remember, if you see an -*ing* word, it might be a verb, or a gerund, or a participle. You have to notice what it is doing in the sentence.

1. **Elucidating** the document was an act of intellect.
   n.   adj.   n.   v.   adj.   n.   prep.   n.
   ----------------------- subj. --------------------   LVP   S.C.   --------prep. phrase--------
   --------------------gerund phrase--------------

2. **Mediating** the dispute, the Germans concurred **affably**.
   adj.   adj.   n.   adj.   n.   v.   adv.
                          subj.   AVP
   -------------participial phrase--------

3. With a **mortifying** sarcasm, Caesar wrote a reply.
   prep.   adj.   adj.   n.   n.   v.   adj.   n.
                          subj.   AVP   D.O.
   ----------------prepositional phrase--------------

4. Preparing **sanguinely**, Caesar was a calming example.

5. **Mediating** disputes was not easy for the Vandal king.

6. The centurion was **importuning** citizens for patience.

7. **Procuring** new supplies, the general shocked the legions.

Here is a four-level analysis of a sentence using the adjective *gratuitous*, which means unfounded, unwarranted, not called for.

	Cicero	delivered	a	diatribe	of	**gratuitous**	insults.
Parts of Speech:	n.	v.	adj.	n.	prep.	adj.	n.
Parts of Sentence:	subj.	AVP		D.O.			
Phrases:						--prepositional phrase--	
Clauses:	one independent clause; a simple declarative sentence						

Here the adjective *gratuitous* modifies the noun *insults*. Does it seem that we keep repeating the same parts of speech? We do because there are only eight kinds of words, and vocabulary consists mainly of learning a good supply of nouns, adjectives, verbs, and adverbs. In this sentence, the prepositional phrase *of gratuitous insults* modifies the noun *diatribe*, so the prepositional phrase is behaving as though it were an adjective.

One of the secrets of advanced vocabulary is knowing how to alter words in order to use them as different parts of speech. Pick one example from each column below, and write a good sentence using it.

noun	adjective	verb	adverb
gratification	gratified	gratify	-
recurrence	recurrent	recur	-
omniscience	omniscient	-	omnisciently
exorbitance	exorbitant	-	exorbitantly
-	gratuitous	-	gratuitously
transmigration	transmigrated	transmigrate	-

HADRIAN STYLE, 120 A.D.
Michael Clay Thompson

Migrating birds a-flying north,
squawking concepts audible,
and Hadrian exhorted us
to courage, laudable.

We styled our hair like Hadrian,
short beard and ringly head,
the emperor's alacrity
for war—tacit, unsaid.

Gratuitous insults by troops
were affable—no harm.
Transcending rank and family,
that alpha-warrior charm.

The Germans in the Teutoburg
would not be so amused
to hear our legions tramping in.
Resistance unexcused.

We'd splash the Rhine some weeks from now,
declaiming every fear,
and keep a close watch on the trees
and sharpen every spear.

In a traditional ballad quatrain, lines one and three do not rhyme, but lines two and four do rhyme. This allows the stanza to reach its perfection in the final syllable.

Photo by Dr. Thomas Milton Kemnitz

SARDINIA AND CORSICA

West of Italy in the Mediterranean Sea are Sardinia and Corsica. Surrounded by sections of the Mediterranean Sea—viz., the Ligurian, Tyrrhenian, and Sardinian Seas—the islands are similar in geography but different in government, one being French and the other Italian. In the ancient world, both islands were settled by Phoenician mariners, who built trading posts there. The islands were then colonized by the Greeks and the Carthaginians. The inexorable Romans annexed both Corsica and Sardinia in the First Punic War, turning the islands into a Roman province for nearly 700 years. During that period, Rome was able to pacify the coastal areas of the islands, but in the heavily forested interiors, the local populations would not be placated and resisted Roman rule. The Romans used the islands as a place to exile bothersome political opponents. It would take many pages to elucidate the complex history of the two islands.

The two islands are separated by the Strait of Bonifacio, named after the Corsican town Bonifacio. The strait is recognized as dangerous water for its unpredictable weather and shallow shoals, and after many disasters, ships that carry dangerous materials are no longer allowed to sail through the strait but must circumvent the islands.

Just ten miles south of Corsica, the rocky island of Sardinia is the second-largest island in the Mediterranean Sea. Sardinia is an autonomous region of Italy. It was a source of grain for Rome during the Roman Republic. It was the location of a number of Stone Age cultures, including the Nuragic civilization, which beginning in 1500 B.C. built strong, round fortresses of stone. The Phoenicians began to arrive in Sardinia in about 1000 B.C. After Roman occupation, Vandals took Sardinia in 456, but the Romans retook the island after about eighty years of Vandal control.

Even though mountainous Corsica lies in close proximity to Sardinia, it is a French island—one of twenty-seven regions of France. Prior to becoming part of France, it was controlled by the Republic of Genoa. Corsica is 114 miles long and fifty-two miles wide. During the Roman Republic, it supplied Rome with wax. In 1769 Napoleon Bonaparte was born in Ajaccio, the capital of Corsica. Corsica has its own singular language, but the culture transcends localized cultural limitations and includes French and Italian elements. Corsica is also famous for its practice of vendetta, a social code that requires the killing of anyone who mortifies a family's honor.

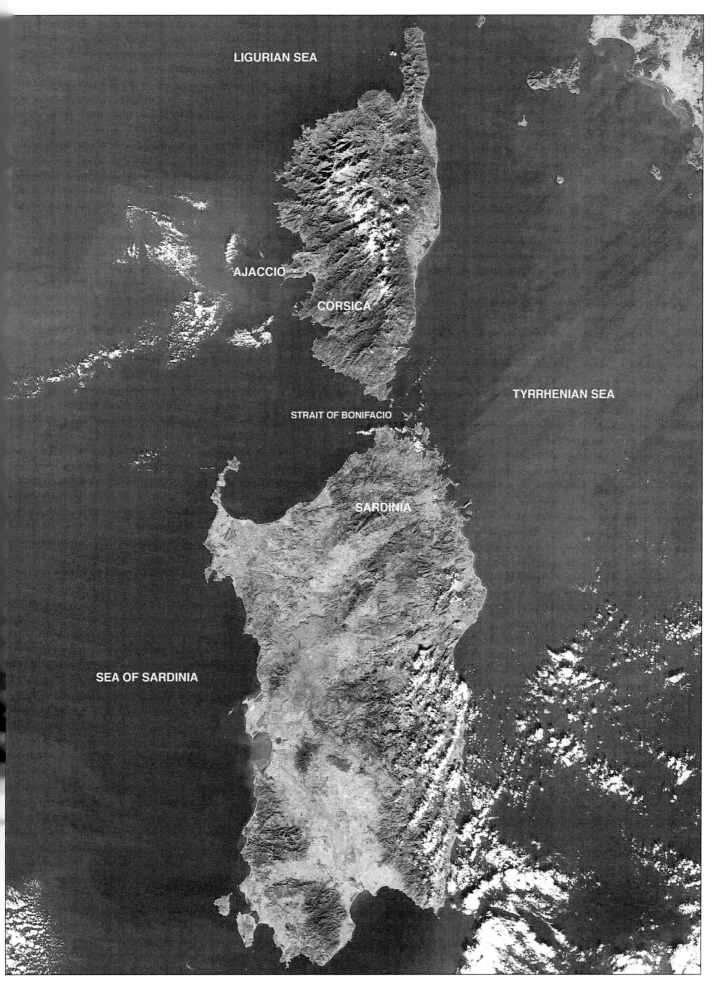

LIGURIAN SEA

AJACCIO

CORSICA

TYRRHENIAN SEA

STRAIT OF BONIFACIO

SARDINIA

SEA OF SARDINIA

REVIEW FOR CUMULATIVE QUIZ

com	together	**vita**	life
intra	within	**vid**	look
cent	one hundred	**pater**	father
ad	to	**matri**	mother
fer	carry	**pop**	people
loco	place	**sur**	over
alter	other	**contra**	against
stell	star	**amat**	love
luna	moon	**greg**	group
clam	cry out	**tang**	touch
mar	sea	**junct**	join
luc	light	**medi**	middle
tempor	time	**grat**	pleasing
curr	run	**trans**	across
migr	wander	**rupt**	break

placate	to appease	**commandeer**	officially take control
derision	ridicule	**intramural**	within an institution
vivacious	full of life	**centennial**	of a 100th anniversary
procure	to acquire	*ad infinitum*	again and again forever
retort	a quick, clever reply	**infer**	conclude from evidence
vitality	strength, energy	**audible**	able to be heard
videlicet (viz.)	namely	**benevolent**	charitable
paternal	of the father	**somber**	gloomy
matriarch	female head of family	**prostrate**	lying flat
populous	densely populated	**profuse**	abundant
localized	restricted to a place	**surfeit**	an excessive amount
altercation	a noisy argument	**contrary**	the opposite
stellar	of a star	**ostentatious**	showy
inexorable	inevitable	**indolent**	lazy
doleful	mournful	**alacrity**	eagerness
amatory	romantic	**sublunar**	under the moon
aggregate	a collected mass	**declaim**	speak against
entangled	snared, involved	**oblique**	indirect or slanting
pensive	thoughtful	**magnanimous**	generous
importune	to pester	**peremptory**	dictatorial
mariner	a sailor	**adjunct**	an unessential addition
elucidate	to explain	**mediate**	to intervene
temporize	to delay	**tacit**	unspoken
affable	friendly	**sanguine**	cheerfully confident
torpid	sluggish	**mortify**	profoundly humiliate
gratuitous	uncalled for	**concur**	to agree
transcend	to go beyond limits	**migratory**	moving seasonally
disruption	a disturbing interruption		

Photo by Dr. Thomas Milton Kemnitz

Roman sculpture
of a barbarian

LESSON XII · CLASSIC WORDS

English	*Spanish*
obsequious: cringing, submissive	*obsequioso*
ignominy: disgrace	*ignominia*
acquiescence: passive compliance	*acquiescencia*
impassive: expressionless, without emotion	*impasible*
impending: about to happen	*pendiente*

OBSEQUIOUS (ob-SEE-kwee-us)

The adjective *obsequious* comes from the Latin *obequiosus*. An obsequious person is a cringing, submissive follower, so over-willing to please that it is repulsive. Joseph Heller, in *Catch-22*, wrote that "he was stricken early with a guilty fear of people and an obsequious impulse to apologize to society for the fact that he was not Henry Fonda." Thornton Wilder wrote in *The Bridge of San Luis Rey* that the "frightened mother became meek and obsequious." In Bram Stoker's *Dracula,* we read that "the urbane undertaker proved that his staff were afflicted—or blessed—with something of his own obsequious suavity." In *Vanity Fair*, Thackeray wrote that the "penniless colonel became quite obsequious and respectful to the head of his house, and despised the milksop Pitt no longer." In Jane Austen's *Pride and Prejudice,* we find "a mixture of pride and obsequiousness, self-importance and humility." Which of these quotes do you think is the best illustration of *obsequious*?

IGNOMINY (IG-noh-man-ee)

The English noun *ignominy* (the adjective is *ignominious*) comes from the Latin *ignominia* and refers to deep humiliation, disgrace, dishonor. In George Orwell's *Animal Farm,* we find that "within five minutes of their invasion they were in ignominious retreat." In Jack London's *White Fang*, "The team dispersed in ignominious defeat." Kenneth Grahame, in *The Wind in the Willows*, described how an animal is "insulted, jeered at, and ignominiously flung into the water." Herman Melville wrote in *Billy Budd* that "a simpleton had, through his very simplicity, ignominiously baffled him." Charlotte Brontë wrote in *Jane Eyre* that the "punishment seemed to me in a high degree ignominious." In *Frankenstein,* Mary Shelley's monster moans that "all looked on me as a wretch doomed to ignominy and perdition." One of the best examples is from Charles Dickens's

Great Expectations, where Pip describes "having my face ignominiously shoved against the kitchen wall."

ACQUIESCENCE (ah-kwee-ESS-ence)

To acquiesce, from the Latin *acquiescere*, is to comply passively and obediently. We understand even better when we learn that *acquiesce* comes from the Latin *quiescere*, to be quiet. It is a relative of the English adjective *quiescent*. In Harper Lee's *To Kill a Mockingbird*, a character is "puzzled by his amiable acquiescence." Thomas Hardy wrote in *Jude the Obscure* that "He passively acquiesced in her wish to go in." In Melville's *Moby Dick,* Ishmael says that "as all my remonstrances produced no effect on Queequeg, I was obliged to acquiesce." Charles Dickens wrote in *David Copperfield* that "I submissively expressed, by my silence, my acquiescence in all I had heard from my superior in years and knowledge." In James Fenimore Cooper's *The Last of the Mohicans*, "The Delaware gravely bowed his acquiescence to what he knew to be false." And Jane Austen used *acquiesce* in *Pride and Prejudice*: "Elizabeth said no more—but her mind could not acquiesce."

IMPASSIVE (im-PASS-iv)

To be impassive, from the Latin *impassibilis*, is to be expressionless and without emotion. In Bernard Malamud's novel *The Natural,* we read that "His rocklike frame was motionless, his face impassive, unsmiling, dark." Pearl Buck wrote in *The Good Earth* that "he had learned now from that impassive square countenance to detect small changes at first invisible to him." Sir Arthur Conan Doyle wrote in *The Hound of the Baskervilles* that "She was a large, impassive, heavy-featured woman with a stern, set expression of mouth." A wonderful example comes from Thomas Hardy's 1878 novel *The Return of the Native*: "Venn sat with lips impassively closed and eyes reduced to a pair of unimportant twinkles." In his great poem *Leaves of Grass,* Walt Whitman referred to the "impassive stones that receive and return so many echoes." And in Charles Dickens's *Hard Times,* we read that "From that moment she was impassive, proud and cold." What do you think Walt Whitman meant in *Leaves of Grass* by the words "black and impassive guns"?

IMPENDING (im-PEN-ding)

The English adjective *impending*, from the Latin *impendere*, refers to things that are about to happen, that are hanging over us. In Orwell's *Animal Farm*, there are "rumors of an impending treacherous attack." In *Why We Can't Wait*, Dr. Martin Luther King, Jr., referred to "the impending crisis." John F. Kennedy wrote in *Profiles in Courage* that "Sam Houston was not one to sit morosely brooding until the whispers of impending defeat were replaced by the avalanche that would crush him." In Jack London's *White Fang,* there is "a feeling as of something terrible impending." Kenneth Grahame wrote in *The Wind in the Willows* that "he cried in despair, plumping down on a seat, with tears impending." A more unusual use of *impending* comes from Stephen Crane in *The Red Badge of Courage*: "An impending splendor could be seen in the eastern sky."

REVIEW WORDS FROM *CAESAR'S ENGLISH I*

vulgar: common
traverse: to cross
undulate: to wave
vivid: bright
pallor: paleness

CAESAR'S MATHEMATICS

VII obsequious attendants approached the Roman emperor. XXIII politicians in ignominy joined them. The emperor was impassive in the face of their importunities until an impending Vandal invasion and the arrival of XLIX disruptive senators forced him to acquiesce. Including the obsequious attendants, the politicians in ignominy, and the disruptive senators, how many people importuned the emperor?

CAESAR'S ESSAY

Write a short essay concerning an important historical figure in Roman history. It could be Caesar, or Augustus, or Brutus, or any other figure. Remember that this is an essay, not a chronological sequence beginning with the person's birth and ending with the death. There must be a topic that you discuss.

CAESAR'S WORD SEARCH

In the puzzle, find the Latin-based English words that you see below. They might be vertical, horizontal, or diagonal. Always notice the stems that are in the words.

T	W	I	W	E	I	D	T	C	O	N	C	U	R	I
O	D	M	I	S	G	I	E	L	B	A	F	F	A	L
B	E	P	M	L	N	P	M	O	R	T	I	F	Y	V
S	F	E	P	E	O	R	P	T	C	N	U	J	D	A
E	D	N	A	F	M	O	O	U	H	N	I	I	O	N
Q	R	D	S	G	I	T	R	A	N	S	C	E	N	D
U	Q	I	S	H	N	O	I	T	P	U	R	S	I	D
I	S	N	I	P	Y	A	Z	G	X	R	Z	Y	J	Y
O	K	G	V	N	M	N	E	N	I	U	G	N	A	S
U	I	C	E	T	O	M	A	R	I	N	E	R	X	T
S	O	Y	A	B	W	K	M	E	D	I	A	T	E	J
T	A	C	Q	U	I	E	S	C	E	N	C	E	K	C
U	I	R	M	I	M	I	G	R	A	T	O	R	Y	H
T	T	F	N	D	G	R	A	T	U	I	T	O	U	S
V	E	T	A	D	I	C	U	L	E	C	L	R	J	K

obsequious	gratuitous	tacit	mariner
ignominy	concur	affable	adjunct
acquiescence	transcend	sanguine	elucidate
impassive	migratory	torpid	mediate
impending	disruption	mortify	temporize

1. Which of these words has the most beautiful sound?
2. Which of these words will you see in novels?
3. Which word is most unusual?
4. Which word is the most scholarly or academic?
5. Which word has the most exact meaning?

CAESAR'S CLASSIC WORDS CHALLENGE

If we want to get a feel for how words are used, we must see how great writers use words. In each case below, one of the choices was the word used by the author. For you, this is a word game. Your challenge is to guess which word the author used. This is not a test; it is a game because more than one word choice may work perfectly well. See if you can use your sensitivity and intuition to guess which word the author used. You may need a dictionary.

1. From Thomas Hardy's *The Return of the Native*

   Venn sat with lips _____ closed.
   - a. acquiescently
   - b. obsequiously
   - c. ignominiously
   - d. impassively

2. From Thornton Wilder's *The Bridge of San Luis Rey*

   It was intended as an _____ flattery to the Condesa, and was untrue.
   - a. ignominious
   - b. obsequious
   - c. impassive
   - d. impending

3. From Joseph Conrad's *Lord Jim*

   Andy shrugged his shoulders, and gave an _____ whistle.
   - a. acquiescent
   - b. ignominious
   - c. impending
   - d. obsequious

CAESAR'S GRAMMAR · PHRASES

The first three sentences below are worked out for you. See if you can solve the next four, identifying the parts of speech, parts of sentence, and phrases for each sentence. Remember, if you see an -*ing* word, it might be a verb, or a gerund, or a participle. You have to notice what it is doing in the sentence.

1. The **obsequious** flattering   gave   Decius   a   headache.
   adj.   adj.   n.   v.   n.   adj.   n.
   -------------------- subj. -------------------- AVP   I.O.   D.O.
   --------------------gerund phrase--------------

2. **Concurring** immediately,   Augustus   **acquiesced**   to   the demand.
   adj.   adv.   n.   v.   prep. adj.   n.
                                            subj.   AVP
   --------------participial phrase----------   ---------prep. phrase--------

3. **Transcending** their imaginations, Augustus planned the construction.
   adj.   adj.   n.   n.   v.   adj.   n.
                                       subj.   AVP   D.O.
   --------------------participial phrase-------------------

4. **Acquiescing** repeatedly   gave   the   emperor   a   low   repute.

5. The **impassive** emperor disliked **importuning** the ambassador.

6. Insulting the king **gratuitously**, Augustus dropped   the   scroll.

7. **Gratuitously mortifying** the crowd was the senator's specialty.

Here is a four-level analysis of a sentence using the adjective *obsequious*, which means cringing, submissive.

	The	**obsequious**	toady	flattered	Caesar	every	day.
Parts of Speech:	adj.	adj.	n.	v.	n.	adj.	n.
Parts of Sentence:			subj.	AVP	D.O.		
Phrases:	no prepositional, appositive, or verbal phrases						
Clauses:	one independent clause; a simple declarative sentence						

Here the adjective *obsequious* modifies the noun *toady*. A toady is a fawning, flattering, submissive person, so it makes sense that a toady would be obsequious. Once again, we see a direct object receiving the action of the action verb.

One of the secrets of advanced vocabulary is knowing how to alter words in order to use them as different parts of speech. Pick one example from each column below, and write a good sentence using it.

noun	adjective	verb	adverb
audibility	audible	-	audibly
benevolence	benevolent	-	benevolently
somberness	somber	-	somberly
prostration	prostrated	prostrate	-
profusion	profuse	-	profusely
serenity	serene	-	serenely
odium	odious	-	odiously

CAESAR'S SESQUIPEDALIAN STORY

The odious, obsequious fool followed the emperor through the arch, ranting about how he venerated his majesty and apologizing for being ignominious. His singular nostrils undulated with acute anxiety as the two men traversed the marble floor, passing the prodigious, ostentatious columns and serene tranquility of the inner doors where Caesar took his repose. With a melancholy visage the fool importuned Caesar inexorably in oblique phrases, but Caesar would not acquiesce. Impassively, Caesar continued placidly down the hall, past the grotesquely affable merchants and manifestly amiable politicians with their tacit agendas. The perplexed fool understood nothing; his incredulous countenance registered only a mortified indolence that did not abate, and he little knew that Caesar, implacable when angered, was about to retort with peremptory, condescending derision, rather than the benevolent and magnanimous altruism he expected. Still the vulgar fool hopped along behind Caesar, clamoring for attention and mistaking Caesar's somber silence for mere pensiveness.

Sabina, c 136 B.C.

Photo by Dr. Thomas Milton Kemnitz

SONNET TO PLOTINA

Michael Clay Thompson

Plotina, pensive, watched Hadrian, her child—
well, her adopted child, with Trajan—
and knew he'd need her savvy and her wiles
to rule Rome-world once he became a man.

No acquiescence would be good enough
for him, no tacit or impassive stoic face.
He'd have to frown like pharaoh, talk gruff,
or some obsequious killer'd take his place.

Benevolence for proletarians of Rome
and schools and education for the poor
were what her Epicurean philosophy had shown
would help Hadrian's authority endure.

Disruptions shook the alpine borders now,
but snow'd begun to shut the passes down.

Plotina

HIBERNIA (IRELAND)

Although there are doleful remains of modest Roman camps in Ireland, as well as findings of ancient Roman artifacts such as coins and pottery, Rome does not appear to have invested heavily in occupying Ireland. According to Tacitus, who called Ireland Hibernia after the Latin *hibernus,* wintry, there was an expedition in 82 A.D. led by general Agricola who apparently crossed the Irish Sea. There is little evidence for the facts of the expedition or information about the mariners. Seneca noted that Agricola believed Hibernia could be conquered by a single Roman legion and some adjuncts, which would mean about 6,000 men. Irish raiders did attack Roman legions in Gaul and Britannia. If these are the high points of Roman involvement with Hibernia, then we can understand why the vitality of Irish culture bears less Latin influence than is the case in other European regions.

The truth is that the Romans knew about Hibernia and undertook minor explorations but little more, resulting in Roman knowledge being limited to vague ideas about Hibernia being cold—too cold to be populous—and inhabited by fierce tribes. The Romans believed that Hibernia lay between Hispania and Brittania.

By the time of the geographer Ptolemy in about 150 A.D., the Romans could finally elucidate details about Irish tribes and geographical features of Hibernia. On the other hand, the Irish histories—written after the introduction of Christianity because prior to that there was no written language in Ireland—do not mention the ignominious Romans.

During the Middle Ages, Irish monasteries devoted time to the copying of Latin manuscripts from the Roman Empire. Monks copied works in Greek and Latin, and some of these copies are the source of our knowledge of classical literature. *The Book of Kells*, an extravagantly illuminated manuscript of the four Gospels, is one of the masterpieces of the genre.

Saint Patrick, born about 387 in Britannia, was captured and taken in slavery to Ireland when he was sixteen years old. He worked as a shepherd and escaped six years later and fled back to England, but he returned to Ireland as a missionary after he joined the clergy. He became the patriarch of Christianity in Ireland. Today Patrick is the patron saint of Ireland. Scholars concur that two letters written by Saint Patrick in Latin have survived.

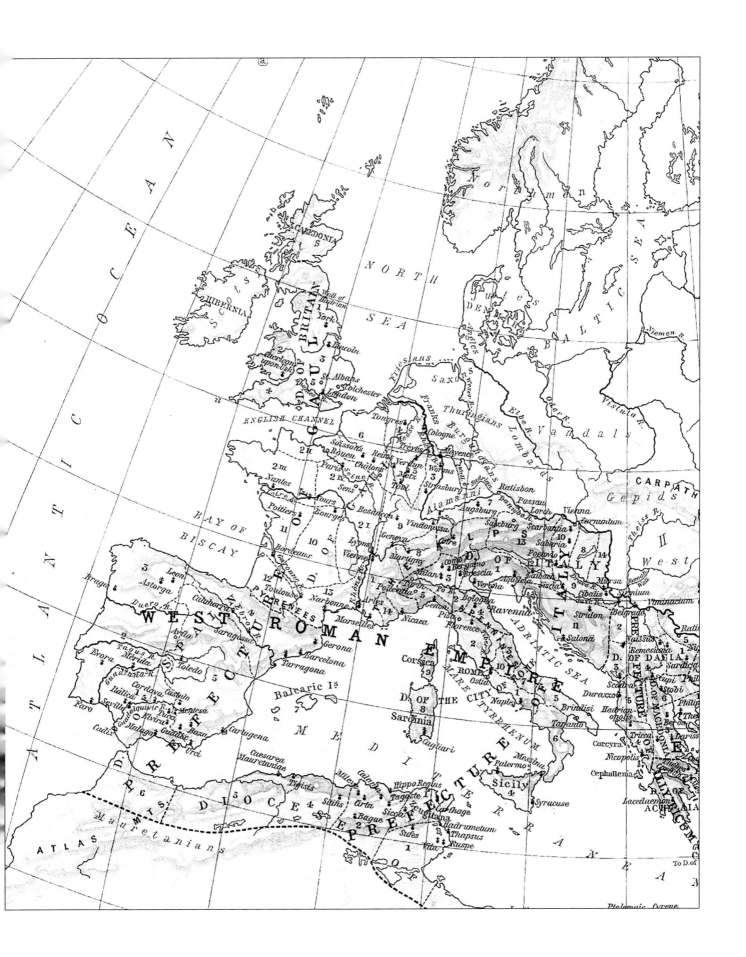

REVIEW FOR CUMULATIVE QUIZ

com	together	**vita**	life
intra	within	**vid**	look
cent	one hundred	**pater**	father
ad	to	**matri**	mother
fer	carry	**pop**	people
loco	place	**sur**	over
alter	other	**contra**	against
stell	star	**amat**	love
luna	moon	**greg**	group
clam	cry out	**tang**	touch
mar	sea	**junct**	join
luc	light	**medi**	middle
tempor	time	**grat**	pleasing
curr	run	**trans**	across
migr	wander	**rupt**	break

placate	to appease	**commandeer**	officially take control
derision	ridicule	**intramural**	within an institution
vivacious	full of life	**centennial**	of a 100th anniversary
procure	to acquire	*ad infinitum*	again and again forever
retort	a quick, clever reply	**infer**	conclude from evidence
vitality	strength, energy	**audible**	able to be heard
videlicet (viz.)	namely	**benevolent**	charitable
paternal	of the father	**somber**	gloomy
matriarch	female head of family	**prostrate**	lying flat
populous	densely populated	**profuse**	abundant
localized	restricted to a place	**surfeit**	an excessive amount
altercation	a noisy argument	**contrary**	the opposite
stellar	of a star	**ostentatious**	showy
inexorable	inevitable	**indolent**	lazy
doleful	mournful	**alacrity**	eagerness
amatory	romantic	**sublunar**	under the moon
aggregate	a collected mass	**declaim**	speak against
entangled	snared, involved	**oblique**	indirect or slanting
pensive	thoughtful	**magnanimous**	generous
importune	to pester	**peremptory**	dictatorial
mariner	a sailor	**adjunct**	an unessential addition
elucidate	to explain	**mediate**	to intervene
temporize	to delay	**tacit**	unspoken
affable	friendly	**sanguine**	cheerfully confident
torpid	sluggish	**mortify**	profoundly humiliate
gratuitous	uncalled for	**concur**	to agree
transcend	to go beyond limits	**migratory**	moving seasonally
disruption	a disturbing interruption	**obsequious**	cringing, submissive
ignominy	disgrace	**acquiescence**	passive compliance
impassive	expressionless, without emotion	**impending**	about to happen

Photo by Dr. Thomas Milton Kemnitz

LESSON XIII · LATIN STEMS

stem	meaning	modern examples	Spanish
clud	close	exclude, included, preclude	*incluido*
se	apart	separate, secede, sedition	*sedición*
plu	more	plus, pluralism, nonplussed	*pluralismo*
germ	vital	germ, germinate, germane	*germinar*
fus	pour	transfusion, infusion, fusillade	*fusilería*

CLUD means close. To *exclude* is to close out, to be *included* is to be admitted, and to *preclude* something that might happen means to stop it, to close the possibility before it happens.

SE means apart. To *separate* is to put something apart; to *secede* is to go apart, as the South did in the Civil War; and *sedition* is inciting people to rebel against the government.

PLU means more. We see *plur* and *plus* versions. A *plus* is an addition of more, *pluralism* is the belief in a society of many different groups, and to be *nonplussed* is to be overwhelmingly confused, feeling like "No more! Tell me no more!"

GERM means vital. A *germ* is a tiny living organism, to *germinate* is to become vital and grow, and a *germane* idea is one that is vital to the conversation.

FUS means pour. In a *transfusion*, blood pours from one person to another; in an *infusion* of ideas, the ideas pour in from elsewhere; and when warships unleash a *fusillade*, there is a great outpouring of gunfire.

REVIEW STEMS FROM *CAESAR'S ENGLISH I*

stem	meaning	modern examples
bene	good	beneficial, benevolent, benign
son	sound	consonant, resonant, assonance
nov	new	innovate, renovate, nova
sangui	blood	sanguine, sanguinary, consanguinity
cogn	know	recognize, cognomen, precognition

municant transfer patricide conclude

osition sedition depopulate matricide

on fusion paternal vitamin transform

nport immigrate transcript patrilineal

or secluded patronize video transitive

ence matrimony interclude germinal

ost provide diffuse segregate effusive

sm vital transmigrate abrupt commix

ive transfix occlude plurality seclude

pulous separate transoceanic suffuse

itude gratuitious patronize germicide

transect populace matrilocal vitalize

neal germane mistranslate germinate

de transmigrate ingratiate repatriated

ice transgression evidence disruptive

oster exclude select nonplussed video

atriated matriarch transfusion diffuse

ratulate preclude transfusion grateful

tural videlicet paternalism migratory

comport secede corruption secession

NONFICTION WORDS

Here are five important nonfiction words. You might not hear them often in daily conversation, but you will encounter them frequently in your future academic life. Each word is based on one of the stems in the lesson.

stem	word	definition
clud	**preclude**	prevent
se	**seclude**	isolate from people
plu	**nonplussed**	confused
germ	**germane**	relevant
fus	**infusion**	an inpouring

PRECLUDE is a verb that means to prevent from happening, to do something in advance that makes something impossible. In Edith Wharton's *Ethan Frome*, we read, "But for the moment his sense of relief was so great as to preclude all other feelings."

SECLUDE is a verb that means to shut away from society, to keep away from other people. Famous scholars often seclude themselves for years in order to write and research.

NONPLUSSED is an adjective that means surprised and confused. It sometimes is spelled *nonplused*. In Herman Melville's great novel *Moby Dick*, a character is "completely nonplussed and confounded about the stranger."

GERMANE is an adjective that means relevant to the topic. If you are being germane, you are sticking to the subject. In Herman Melville's *Billy Budd*, we read that "nothing especially germane to the story occurred."

INFUSION is a noun that refers to the inpouring of a new element. In Kate Chopin's novel *The Awakening*, we read that "She was an American woman, with a small infusion of French, which seemed to have been lost in dilution."

Write two good sentences for each word.

SECLUDE

CAESAR'S ANALOGIES: Find the most similar pairs.

PRECLUDE : AVOID ::
    a. secede : withdraw
    b. seed : germinate
    c. exclude : include
    d. blood : transfusion

GUNS : FUSILLADE ::
    a. separate : unify
    b. germane : relevant
    c. exclude : barriers
    d. tubes : transfusion

CAESAR'S ANTONYMS: Find the best opposite.

NONPLUSSED
    a. germane
    b. lucid
    c. infused
    d. precluded

SEDITION
    a. exclusion
    b. patriotism
    c. germination
    d. treachery

CAESAR'S CONTEXT: Find the best word to complete the sentence.

After the insurrection, new ideas began to _____.
    a. fusillade
    b. secede
    c. germinate
    d. include

No province was permitted to _____ from the Empire.
    a. renovate
    b. preclude
    c. germinate
    d. secede

In the panic of the barbarian assault, the legion commander was _____.
    a. nonplussed
    b. separate
    c. germane
    d. transfused

CAESAR'S MATHEMATICS

The emperor precluded the invasion by destroying the bridges over the Rhine. XIV barbarian tribes were nonplussed by the tactic and did not invade. XXVII other tribes secluded themselves in remote mountain valleys in order to think. They did not invade either. XXXII tribes retreated from the border in obsequious ignominy and did not invade. XXI tribes found germane military responses to the problem, and one third of them continued their invasions. How many tribes did not invade across the border into the Roman Empire?

CAESAR'S ESSAY

In an academic essay, great care must be given to the graceful transition from one paragraph to the next. It is usually best to avoid mechanical, stiff, boring transitions such as "First," "Second," and so forth, and it is always best to avoid the dreaded -ly terms such as *firstly* and *secondly,* which sound pedantic and pretentious. Instead, use graceful topic sentences for your paragraphs that connect the previous paragraph to the present paragraph. For this purpose, a D,I complex sentence beginning with a dependent clause often works beautifully. An example:

> The winter, with its snow and freezing winds, forced an end to the hostilities. The rivers had frozen, but the tribes could not cross the ice to invade because it would mean extended exposure to severe winter conditions. The tribes settled down to wait until the weather made a new invasion possible.
>
> When the winter ended, the spring brought new conditions that made the assembling, equipping, and training of an army possible. The tribes began to gather in a mountain recess to create the greatest invasion force that they had yet assembled.

Write a short essay, concentrating on the quality of the topic sentences that establish the graceful flow of the essay.

CAESAR'S WORD SEARCH

In the puzzle, find the Latin-based English words that you see below. They might be vertical, horizontal, or diagonal. Always notice the stems that are in the words.

Q	P	R	C	K	Y	R	A	N	I	U	G	N	A	S
N	N	S	B	F	D	I	S	S	O	N	A	N	T	G
P	L	O	E	W	L	L	D	I	K	E	J	Q	S	H
P	F	X	N	N	I	V	E	D	E	C	E	S	F	D
R	Z	A	E	P	O	M	W	E	D	E	U	E	R	Y
E	D	E	D	C	L	I	P	Y	N	O	T	W	R	N
C	E	V	I	O	B	U	S	E	I	A	O	B	S	I
L	G	I	C	N	E	S	S	U	N	D	M	F	E	M
U	R	S	T	C	R	R	Q	S	F	D	H	R	G	O
D	A	S	I	U	A	E	T	Y	E	N	I	U	E	N
E	G	A	O	R	S	D	R	F	G	D	I	N	H	G
S	E	P	N	B	J	E	D	U	L	C	E	S	G	I
S	J	M	O	B	T	W	E	Y	T	E	U	Q	Y	U
Z	I	I	A	M	G	R	A	T	U	I	T	O	U	S
A	C	Q	U	I	E	S	C	E	N	C	E	I	I	O

preclude   secede   obsequious   gratuitous
seclude   impending   benediction   concur
nonplussed   impassive   sanguinary   ignominy
germane   acquiescence   dissonant   infusion

1. Which of these words is the most interesting?
2. Which of these words will you use most often?
3. Which two words are related to each other in some way?
4. Which word sounds most scholarly or academic?
5. Which word has the most precise meaning?

CAESAR'S CLASSIC WORDS CHALLENGE

If we want to get a feel for how words are used, we must see how great writers use words. In each case below, one of the choices was the word used by the author. For you, this is a word game. Your challenge is to guess which word the author used. This is not a test; it is a game because more than one word choice may work perfectly well. See if you can use your sensitivity and intuition to guess which word the author used. You may need a dictionary.

1. From Herman Melville's *Billy Budd*

    Nothing especially _____ to the story occurred.
       a. separate
       b. precluded
       c. germane
       d. nonplussed

2. From Edith Wharton's *Ethan Frome*

    His sense of relief was so great as to _____ all other feelings.
       a. separate
       b. transfuse
       c. germinate
       d. preclude

3. From Herman Melville's *Billy Budd*

    He was _____, evincing a confusion.
       a. germane
       b. nonplussed
       c. included
       d. pluralistic

CAESAR'S GRAMMAR · PHRASES

The first three sentences below are worked out for you. See if you can solve the next four, identifying the parts of speech, parts of sentence, and phrases for each sentence. Remember, if you see an -*ing* word, it might be a verb, or a gerund, or a participle. You have to notice what it is doing in the sentence.

1. Introducing   an   **infusion**   of   ideas,   the   Vandals   brought   strength.
    adj.   adj.   n.   prep. n.   adj.   n.   v.   n.
                                                            subj.   AVP   D.O.

    ------------participial phrase-----------   ---prep. phrase--

2. Shocking   the   **nonplussed**   Gauls   was   Caesar's   intention.
    n.   adj.   adj.   n.   v.   n.   n.
    ----------------------------subj.----------------------   LVP   S.C.
    ----------------------gerund phrase--------------------

3. Decius   enjoyed   making   the   most   **germane**   comments.
    n.   v.   n.   adj. adv.   adj.   n.
    subj.   AVP   -----------------------------------D.O.----------------------------------
                       ---------------------------------gerund phrase-----------------------------

4. Building   the   huge   wall   **precluded**   the   invasions   from   Caledonia.

5. **Secluding**   himself   entirely,   Virgil   worked   on   the   poem.

6. Watching   the   **migratory**   birds   gave   Lucius   a   feeling   of   serenity.

7. Creating   **altercations**   and   **disruptions**,   the conspirator   distracted   him.

Here is a four-level analysis of a sentence using the adjective *nonplussed*, which means perplexed, confused.

	When the generals refused, Caesar was truly **nonplussed**.

Parts of Speech:	conj.	adj.	n.	v.	n.	v.	adv.	adj.

Parts of Sentence:		subj.	AVP	subj.	LVP	S.C.

Phrases: no prepositional, appositive, or verbal phrases

Clauses: ------dependent clause------ --------independent clause--------
a D,I complex declarative sentence

In this sentence, the adjective *nonplussed* modifies the noun *Caesar*; this example shows us how an adjective can be a subject complement, modifying its target noun through the linking verb. The sentence also shows us how a complex sentence is made of a dependent clause and an independent clause.

One of the secrets of advanced vocabulary is knowing how to alter words in order to use them as different parts of speech. Pick one example from each column below, and write a good sentence using it.

noun	adjective	verb	adverb
germaneness	germane	-	-
germination	germinated	germinate	-
amiability	amiable	-	amiably
benevolence	benevolent	-	benevolently

POMPEII, 24 AUG., 79 A.D.
Michael Clay Thompson

Somber thunder under the mountain audible,
black blast fast impending, rising wave of burial,
we pause, ignominious, fear-nonplussed, obsequiously
importuning gods to please preclude our doom,
oblique explosions, nosedive fusillades of lava,
the burn-storm now halfway across the bay,
inexorable, ocean shaking, buildings crumbling
in heaving disruption, and the first hail of ash
falling straight down, dusk-cloud of ash hanging
above us, lost crowd of terror-people clamoring
for who-knows-what, words choked, ash-smothered.
Eyes dilated in tacit incredulity, no stupid sanguine
perky confidence remains, no tricks, no time
for affable good-jobs today, no time at all.
Time's up. The universe is blowing apart.
Disgruntled monster-mountain, viz., Vesuvius,
has turned indignant 'gainst our cities populous.
There's no retort, no reasoning with volcanos.
Objection's not germane to plummets of fire.
Jillion tons blown to the stratosphere,
a Hades-continent falling on our world,
filling streets, submerging roofs, a rising surge
of burning stone and burying ash, a city going, sinking—gone,
Titanic town: Pompeii, a gray desert like the moon,
acquiesces helpless in its volcano-tomb,
fading to 1,500 years of shut-eye.
G'night, you sleepy-heads.

NAPLES

HERCULANEUM

POMPEII

GULF OF NAPLES

GULF OF SALERNO

VESUVIUS

On Italy's west coast, 136 miles southeast of Rome on the Gulf of Naples, is Mount Vesuvius, one of the most dangerous volcanos in the world. It is the epicenter of the world's most densely populous volcanic area, with more than 3,000,000 people living in its shadow. In an eruption during the Roman Empire in 79 A.D., the cone-shaped Vesuvius exploded violently, killing tens of thousands of Romans and completely burying the Roman cities of Pompeii and Herculaneum so deeply that their locations could not be discovered for 1,500 years. They are still being unearthed by archeologists today.

Vesuvius is more than 4,200 feet high—about fourteen vertical football fields. It looms over Naples, nine miles to its west, and other cities in its immediate vicinity. It is a stratovolcano, meaning that it is composed of strata: layers of lava, pumice, ash, and other materials that have formed the mountain during its previous explosions. The other most famous stratovolcano in the world is Indonesia's Krakatoa, famous for its catastrophic eruption in 1883. Krakatoa produced the loudest sound the world has ever known—a roar audible as far away as Africa and Perth, Australia.

Vesuvius is still an active volcano; it has erupted repeatedly throughout history, including within the last century. To elucidate the level of danger involved, we will enumerate that after the eruption in 79 A.D., Vesuvius erupted (or probably erupted) in 172, 203, 222, 303, 379, 472, 512, 536, 685, 787, 860, 900, 968, 991, 999, 1006, 1037, 1049, 1073, 1139, 1150, 1270, 1347, 1500, 1631, six times in the 1700s, eight times in the 1800s, in 1906, 1929, and 1944. Although nothing can be done to preclude future danger, volcanologists study Vesuvius in an attempt to infer evidence of impending eruptions for the Italian population.

When Vesuvius exploded in 79 A.D., it sent a cloud of death twenty miles into the air, an aggregate of ash and poisonous fumes that settled down over Italy. Pompeii was one of the towns most proximate to the blast. A Roman town of 20,000 residents, Pompeii was buried under twenty feet of ash and pumice. Its artifacts lay undisturbed for two millennia, making Pompeii one of the best sources of Roman artifacts and other details of Roman life. Scientists have found cavities in the ashes that are in the shape of the bodies of the Roman citizens who died during the eruption.

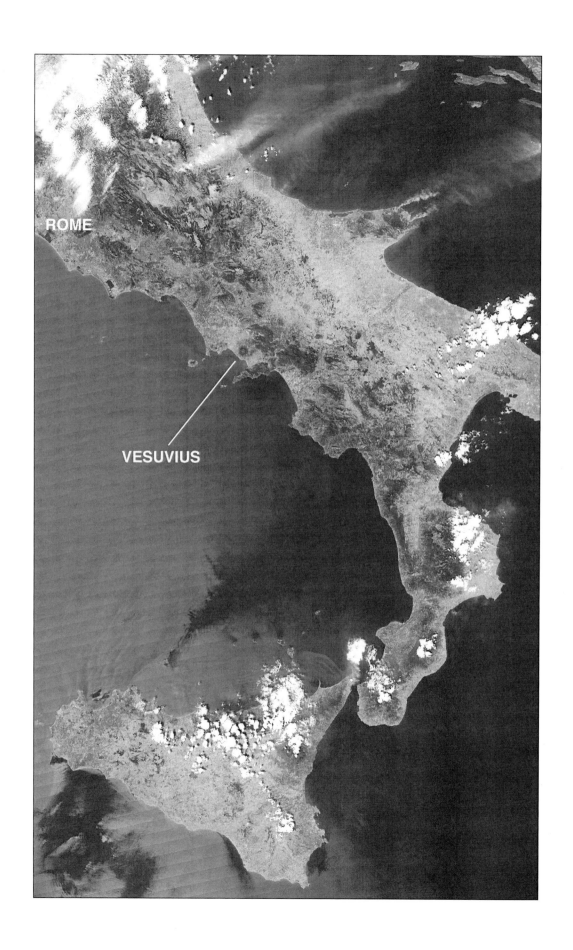

ROME

VESUVIUS

225

REVIEW FOR CUMULATIVE QUIZ

com	together	vita	life
intra	within	vid	look
cent	one hundred	pater	father
ad	to	matri	mother
fer	carry	pop	people
loco	place	sur	over
alter	other	contra	against
stell	star	amat	love
luna	moon	greg	group
clam	cry out	tang	touch
mar	sea	junct	join
luc	light	medi	middle
tempor	time	grat	pleasing
curr	run	trans	across
migr	wander	rupt	break
clud	close	se	apart
plu	more	germ	vital
fus	pour		

placate	to appease	commandeer	officially take control
derision	ridicule	intramural	within an institution
vivacious	full of life	centennial	of a 100th anniversary
procure	to acquire	*ad infinitum*	again and again forever
retort	a quick, clever reply	infer	conclude from evidence
vitality	strength, energy	audible	able to be heard
videlicet (viz.)	namely	benevolent	charitable
paternal	of the father	somber	gloomy
matriarch	female head of family	prostrate	lying flat
populous	densely populated	profuse	abundant
localized	restricted to a place	surfeit	an excessive amount
altercation	a noisy argument	contrary	the opposite
stellar	of a star	ostentatious	showy
inexorable	inevitable	indolent	lazy
doleful	mournful	alacrity	eagerness
amatory	romantic	sublunar	under the moon
aggregate	a collected mass	declaim	speak against
entangled	snared, involved	oblique	indirect or slanting
pensive	thoughtful	magnanimous	generous
importune	to pester	peremptory	dictatorial
mariner	a sailor	adjunct	an unessential addition
elucidate	to explain	mediate	to intervene
temporize	to delay	tacit	unspoken
affable	friendly	sanguine	cheerfully confident
torpid	sluggish	mortify	profoundly humiliate
gratuitous	uncalled for	concur	to agree
transcend	to go beyond limits	migratory	moving seasonally
disruption	a disturbing interruption	obsequious	cringing, submissive
ignominy	disgrace	acquiescence	passive compliance
impassive	expressionless, without emotion	impending	about to happen
preclude	prevent	seclude	isolate from people
nonplussed	confused	germane	relevant
infusion	an inpouring		

Mount Vesuvius, seen from an excavated street in Pompeii

Photo by Dr. Thomas Milton Kemnitz

227

All that is mine,
I carry with me.

- Cicero

LESSON XIV · CLASSIC WORDS

English	*Spanish*
verdure: vegetation	*verdor*
equivocal: ambiguous	*equívoco*
orthodox: traditional	*ortodoxo*
profane: irreverent	*profano*
tumult: disturbance	*tumulto*

VERDURE (VUR-dyoor)

The English noun *verdure*, from the Latin *viridis*, refers to vegetation, to greenery. The adjective form is *verdant*. In *All the King's Men,* Robert Penn Warren wrote that "you hear the July flies grinding away in the verdure." In *Rebecca of Sunnybrook Farm,* Kate Douglass Wiggin wrote that there were "fascinating hollows and hillocks, as well as verdant levels, on which to build houses." Thoreau wrote in *Walden* that "the skunk-cabbage still put forth with perennial verdure." In *Moby Dick,* Herman Melville observed "the spring verdure peeping forth even beneath February's snow." Charlotte Brontë described "a great hill-hollow, rich in verdure and shadow" in *Jane Eyre.* Mary Shelley wrote in *Frankenstein* that "A serene sky and verdant fields filled me with ecstasy." Here is a challenging sentence to understand: in his 1876 novel *The American,* Henry James wrote that "she was not simply taking pity on his aesthetic verdancy." Can you work out what that means, perhaps with the help of a dictionary?

EQUIVOCAL (ee-KWIV-o-cul)

To be *equivocal* (an adjective, from the Latin *aequivocus*) is to be ambiguous, to say or suggest two things at the same time, perhaps intentionally so as to avoid taking a stand. It is to give equal (*equi*) voice (*voc*) to both sides. The verb form is *equivocate*, and the noun is *equivocation*. We also often see the negative form, *unequivocal*, which is what you are when you do take a stand. We find "he cannot equivocate, he cannot delay" in John F. Kennedy's *Profiles in Courage.* In Melville's *Moby Dick*, we find "Claggart's equivocal words." In *The Last of the Mohicans,* James Fenimore Cooper wrote that "the fiercest of human passions was already succeeded by the most profound and unequivocal demonstrations of grief." In *Emma,* Jane Austen wrote, "Your meaning must be unequivocal." Perhaps the most famous *equivocal* sentence comes from William

Shakespeare's 1606 play *Macbeth*: "Faith, here's an equivocator that could swear in both the scales against either scale." What do you think that means?

ORTHODOX (ORTH-o-dox)

The English adjective *orthodox* comes from the Latin *orthodoxus*, which the Romans got from the Greek *orthodoxos*. To be orthodox is to be traditional or conventional in your views, to believe what society expects you to, to have your opinion (*dox*) straight (*ortho*) in the eyes of others. Authority can be suspicious of unorthodoxy, as we see in George Orwell's *1984*: "Another year, two years, and they would be watching her night and day for symptoms of unorthodoxy." John F. Kennedy, in *Profiles in Courage*, wrote that "any unpopular or unorthodox course arouses a storm of protests." In Aldous Huxley's *Brave New World,* a character goes "out of his way to show himself strong and unorthodox," and there is a reference to "All the people who aren't satisfied with orthodoxy, who've got independent ideas of their own." In *Moby Dick,* Herman Melville wrote that "there were some sceptical Greeks and Romans, who, standing out from the orthodox pagans of their times, equally doubted the story of Hercules and the whale." What does being sceptical have to do with being orthodox?

PROFANE (pro-FAIN)

The English adjective *profane*, from the Latin *profanus*, means irreverent, unholy. It can even mean defiled. In *Why We Can't Wait*, Martin Luther King, Jr., wrote that "the word 'compromise' is profane and pernicious." Stephen Crane, in *The Red Badge of Courage*, referred to a soldier's "profane allusions to a general." In Mark Twain's *Tom Sawyer*, "a maidservant's discordant voice profaned the holy calm." Frederick Douglass, in his famous *Narrative*, says that Mr. Plummer was "a profane swearer, and a savage monster." Sir Walter Scott described "a profane quarrel" in *Ivanhoe*. In *Uncle Tom's Cabin*, Harriet Beecher Stowe referred to "various profane expressions, which not even the desire to be graphic in our account shall induce us to transcribe." And in James Fenimore Cooper's *The Last of the Mohicans,* one character observes, "I apprehend that he is rather addicted to profane song."

TUMULT (TUM-ult)

The English noun *tumult*, from the Latin *tumultus*, means a disturbance and traces back to the Latin verb *tumere*, to swell. A tumult is a disturbance that suddenly swells up, a sudden uproar and clamor. Martin Luther King, Jr., recalled "the erupting tumult and catastrophe in the streets of the city" in *Why We Can't Wait*. There is a "prolonged and tumultuous argument" in F. Scott Fitzgerald's *The Great Gatsby*. In Kenneth Grahame's *The Wind in the Willows*, the animals can "hear the tumultuous applause." In *The War of the Worlds*, H.G. Wells described the "tumultuous breathing of the lungs in a strange atmosphere." The pitiful monster in Mary Shelley's *Frankenstein* feels that "their feelings were serene and peaceful, while mine became every day more tumultuous." And Benjamin Franklin wrote in his *Autobiography* that "There was no appeasing the tumult, and we retired to our lodging." In what way is a tumult like a swelling?

REVIEW WORDS FROM *CAESAR'S ENGLISH I*

wistful: yearning
subtle: slight
sagacity: wisdom
remonstrate: to object
tedious: boring

CAESAR'S MATHEMATICS

LXXXIV Roman citizens gathered in the street, looking for fun. XXV of them were indolent and torpid and could not be bothered to take action. XII of them were mortified about something and went home. IX of them went aside to importune the baker for free bread. Of those who remained in the group, half grew pensive and did not want to talk, and the rest continued on, looking for fun. How many Roman citizens kept looking for fun?

EQUIVOCAL

CAESAR'S WORD SEARCH

In the puzzle, find the Latin-based English words that you see below. They might be vertical, horizontal, or diagonal. Always notice the stems that are in the words.

V	E	R	G	R	A	T	U	I	T	O	U	S	J	E
S	R	T	E	I	M	P	E	N	D	I	N	G	U	T
R	G	S	C	W	I	O	B	A	C	Q	O	N	Y	T
U	T	U	M	U	L	T	Y	T	Y	S	N	E	N	H
C	D	O	R	T	H	O	D	O	X	F	P	X	I	E
N	O	I	S	U	F	N	I	G	O	G	L	Y	M	V
O	S	U	W	T	O	P	W	R	D	H	U	J	O	I
C	E	Q	U	I	V	O	C	A	L	I	S	Z	N	S
D	N	E	C	S	N	A	R	T	H	O	S	U	G	S
C	I	S	E	N	A	F	O	R	P	N	E	M	I	A
O	G	B	Q	Y	P	R	E	C	L	U	D	E	K	P
N	A	O	B	V	E	R	D	U	R	E	E	V	M	M
S	E	C	L	U	D	E	U	A	R	A	S	P	B	I
W	E	C	N	E	C	S	E	I	U	Q	C	A	M	E
E	G	E	K	T	E	S	E	N	A	M	R	E	G	I

verdure	preclude	obsequious	gratuitous
equivocal	seclude	ignominy	concur
orthodox	nonplussed	acquiescence	transcend
profane	germane	impassive	impending
tumult	infusion		

1. Which of these words has the most beautiful sound?
2. Which of these words will you see in novels?
3. Which word is most unusual?
4. Which word is the most scholarly or academic?
5. Which word has the most exact meaning?

CAESAR'S CLASSIC WORDS CHALLENGE

If we want to get a feel for how words are used, we must see how great writers use words. In each case below, one of the choices was the word used by the author. For you, this is a word game. Your challenge is to guess which word the author used. This is not a test; it is a game because more than one word choice may work perfectly well. See if you can use your sensitivity and intuition to guess which word the author used. You may need a dictionary.

1. From Aldous Huxley's *Brave New World*

No offense is so heinous as _____ of behaviour.
   a. verdure
   b. equivocation
   c. unorthodoxy
   d. tumult

2. From Arthur Conan Doyle's *The Hound of the Baskervilles*

He was a most wild, _____, and godless man.
   a. profane
   b. orthodox
   c. tumultuous
   d. equivocal

3. From Jane Austen's *Pride and Prejudice*

His answers were at the same time so vague and _____.
   a. profane
   b. orthodox
   c. equivocal
   d. tumultuous

CAESAR'S GRAMMAR · PHRASES

The first three sentences below are worked out for you. See if you can solve the next four, identifying the parts of speech, parts of sentence, and phrases for each sentence. Remember, if you see an -*ing* word, it might be a verb, or a gerund, or a participle. You have to notice what it is doing in the sentence.

1. Watching   the   **tumult**   was   causing   a   problem.
    n.   adj.   n.   v.   v.   adj.   n.
    ---------------------subj.--------------   ---------AVP--------   D.O.
    ----------------gerund phrase------------

2. The   **profane**   centurion   enjoyed   offending   his   pals.
    adj.   adj.   n.   v.   n.   adj.   n.
                         subj.   AVP   ----------------D.O.----------------
                                          ----------gerund phrase----------

3. Promoting   **orthodox**   ideas,   the   emperor   traveled   through Gaul.
    adj.   adj.   n.   adj.   n.   v.   prep.   n.
                                          subj.   AVP
    ----------------participial phrase----------------   -----prep. phrase-----

4. Cutting   the   **verdure**   down,   the   legions   built   their   camp.

5. Giving   an   **equivocal**   answer   was   his   abrupt   retort.

6. Giving   a   **germane**   answer,   Theodora   **precluded**   further   comment.

7. The   **nonplussed**   centurion   gave   Decius   an   answer.

Here is a four-level analysis of a sentence using the adjective *equivocal*, which means ambiguous, giving equal voice to both sides of a question.

	Caesar	was	**equivocal**,	and	they	hesitated	circumspectly.
Parts of Speech:	n.	v.	adj.	conj.	pron.	v.	adv.

Parts of Sentence:	subj.	LVP	S.C.		subj.	AVP	

Phrases: no prepositional, appositive, or verbal phrases

Clauses: ----independent clause----   -------independent clause-------
an I,ccI compound declarative sentence

In this sentence, the adjective *equivocal* modifies the noun *Caesar* as the subject complement linked to its noun by a linking verb. This sentence is a classic I,ccI compound sentence, made of two independent clauses joined by a coordinating conjunction.

One of the secrets of advanced vocabulary is knowing how to alter words in order to use them as different parts of speech. Pick one example from each column below, and write a good sentence using it.

noun	adjective	verb	adverb
equivocation	equivocal	equivocate	equivocally
orthodoxy	orthodox	-	-
tumult	tumultuous	-	tumultuously
profanity	profane	profane	profanely
remonstration	-	remonstrate	-
sagacity	sagacious	-	sagaciously
wistfulness	wistful	-	wistfully
veneration	venerable	venerate	-

GLADIATORS
Michael Clay Thompson

The Romans pulled them through the streets in carts.
Quintus swallowed profane curses as the wooden
wheels clacked on the stones. Publius Varus had sold
him to this fate, to die a gladiator. In four days
they would reach the colosseum.

The Romans dragged them through the dark verdure
of the forest in carts, wheels slogging in mud.
Quintus looked at the others, the Numidian and the Goth guy.
In the tumult of the ring, he could take the Goth guy.
The Numidian stared back at Quintus, a retort of eyes,
face impassive—not obsequious, not a bit. In three days
they would reach the colosseum.

The Romans rolled them in ignominy through
the streets, vulgar crowds hurling gratuitous slurs,
altercations breaking out, the clamor of disruption
waking torpid bozos from their dozes.
Quintus felt equivocal about his week.
He'd have to kill a fellow glad—the Numidian?—
in two days in the colosseum.

With peremptory guffaws, the Romans hauled them quickly
through the ostentatious streets, the clunks of wheels
a rocky credo for the path inexorable to the colosseum.
Quintus glanced at the others, the Numidian and the Goth guy,
the Gaul and some doleful country bloke from Macedon.
Quintus felt a strange alacrity for the fight—
tomorrow—in the colosseum.

Anger is a
short madness.

- Cicero

Photo by Dr. Thomas Milton Kemnitz

THE HELLESPONT (DARDANELLES)

The modern strait of the Dardanelles, which the ancient Greeks named the Hellespont, is a narrow strait in Turkey that connects the Aegean Sea to the Sea of Marmara. The strategic importance of the strait cannot be overstated because it allows ships to sail from anywhere in the Mediterranean up through the Aegean Sea, through the Dardanelles, into the Sea of Marmara, through the Bosporus, past Constantinople/Istanbul, and into the 168,500-square-mile enormity of the Black Sea. It is a kind of natural European Panama Canal or Suez Canal. Viewed in reverse, the Dardanelles allows all of the nations on the Black Sea maritime access to the Aegean, the Mediterranean, and the Atlantic. Because of the Dardanelles, in other words, the Black Sea is not secluded from the other seas of the world.

The dimensions of the Dardanelles are germane: the strait is thirty-eight miles long but less than four miles wide at its widest point, and its maximum depth is less than 350 feet, making it more like a river than an extension of the ocean. The narrow dimensions and the strong currents of the strait make it dangerous to mariners, challenging the inexorable demands of commerce.

The Dardanelles were important in ancient history, being close to Troy and playing an important role in the tumultuous wars between Alexander the Great of Macedon and Darius, the king of the Persian Empire. Xerxes built pontoon bridges across the Dardanelles in order to invade Greece; when a storm destroyed the bridges, disrupting his invasion, he had the water whipped for insolence.

In modern times the Dardanelles have been important to the Byzantines, to Napoleon, to Russia and Great Britain, to the Ottomans, and to other powers. In 1915 and 1916 the horrific Gallipoli campaign was fought on the Gallipoli peninisula between Turkey and a combined force of the British and French, with Turkey emerging victorious.

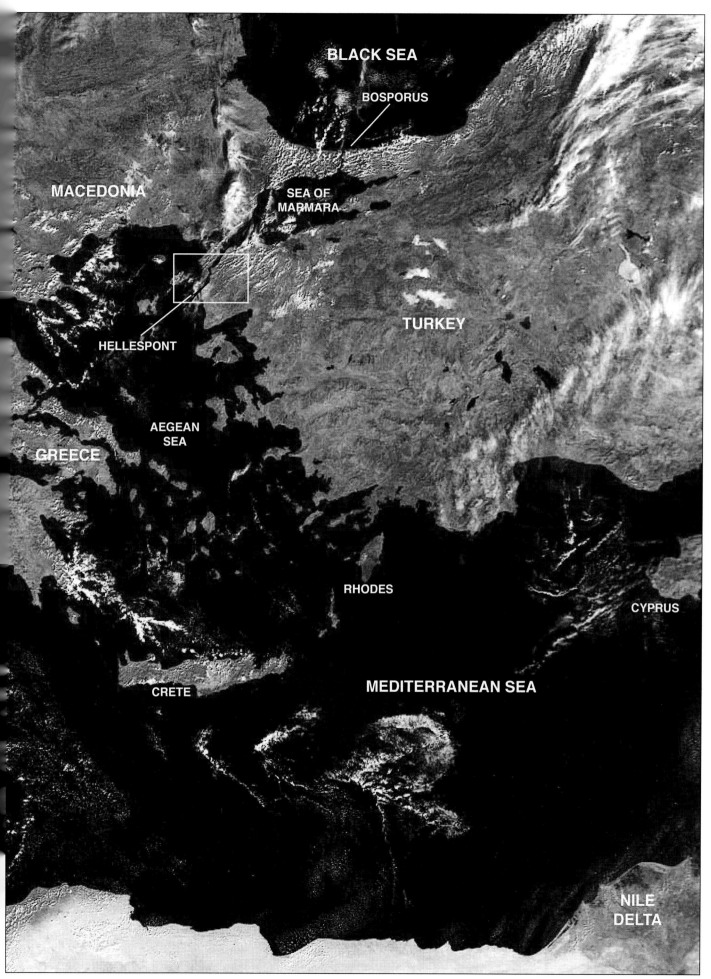

BLACK SEA

BOSPORUS

MACEDONIA

SEA OF
MARMARA

HELLESPONT

TURKEY

AEGEAN
SEA

GREECE

RHODES

CYPRUS

CRETE

MEDITERRANEAN SEA

NILE
DELTA

REVIEW FOR CUMULATIVE QUIZ

com	together	vita	life
intra	within	vid	look
cent	one hundred	pater	father
ad	to	matri	mother
fer	carry	pop	people
loco	place	sur	over
alter	other	contra	against
stell	star	amat	love
luna	moon	greg	group
clam	cry out	tang	touch
mar	sea	junct	join
luc	light	medi	middle
tempor	time	grat	pleasing
curr	run	trans	across
migr	wander	rupt	break
clud	close	se	apart
plu	more	germ	vital
fus	pour		

placate	to appease	commandeer	officially take control
derision	ridicule	intramural	within an institution
vivacious	full of life	centennial	of a 100th anniversary
procure	to acquire	*ad infinitum*	again and again forever
retort	a quick, clever reply	infer	conclude from evidence
vitality	strength, energy	audible	able to be heard
videlicet (viz.)	namely	benevolent	charitable
paternal	of the father	somber	gloomy
matriarch	female head of family	prostrate	lying flat
populous	densely populated	profuse	abundant
localized	restricted to a place	surfeit	an excessive amount
altercation	a noisy argument	contrary	the opposite
stellar	of a star	ostentatious	showy
inexorable	inevitable	indolent	lazy
doleful	mournful	alacrity	eagerness
amatory	romantic	sublunar	under the moon
aggregate	a collected mass	declaim	speak against
entangled	snared, involved	oblique	indirect or slanting
pensive	thoughtful	magnanimous	generous
importune	to pester	peremptory	dictatorial
mariner	a sailor	adjunct	an unessential addition
elucidate	to explain	mediate	to intervene
temporize	to delay	tacit	unspoken
affable	friendly	sanguine	cheerfully confident
torpid	sluggish	mortify	profoundly humiliate
gratuitous	uncalled for	concur	to agree
transcend	to go beyond limits	migratory	moving seasonally
disruption	a disturbing interruption	obsequious	cringing, submissive
ignominy	disgrace	acquiescence	passive compliance
impassive	expressionless, without emotion	impending	about to happen
preclude	prevent	seclude	isolate from people
nonplussed	confused	germane	relevant
infusion	an inpouring	verdure	vegetation
equivocal	ambiguous	orthodox	traditional
profane	irreverent	tumult	disturbance

Photo by Dr. Thomas Milton Kemnitz

Nothing requires the architect's care more than the due proportions of buildings.

- Vitruvius

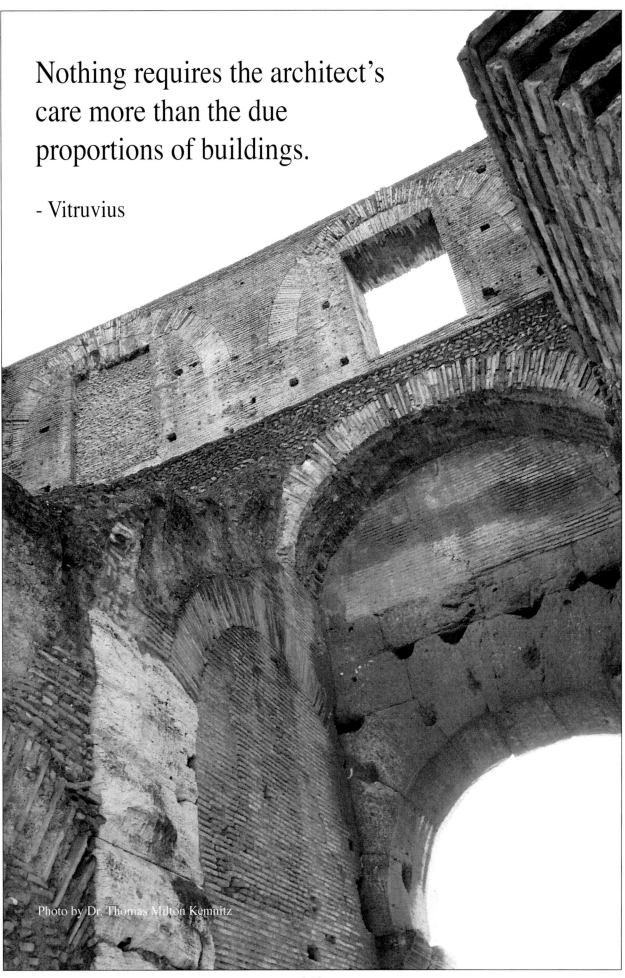

Photo by Dr. Thomas Milton Kemnitz

LESSON XV · LATIN STEMS

stem	meaning	modern examples	Spanish
culp	blame	culprit, culpable, exculpate	*culpable*
pugn	fight	pugnacious, pugilist, oppugn	*pugnaz*
urb	city	urban, suburb, urbane	*urbano*
numer	number	numeral, enumerate, supernumerary	*enumeración*
acr	sharp	acrid, acerbity, acrimony	*acrimonia*

CULP means blame. We blame the *culprit*, to be *culpable* is to be guilty, and to *exculpate* someone is to free him or her from blame.

PUGN means fight. A *pugnacious* person is combative, a *pugilist* is a fighter, and to *oppugn* something is to attack or resist it.

URB means city. An *urban* environment is a city environment, the *suburbs* are the neighborhoods around the city, and an *urbane* person is sophisticated and citified.

NUMER means number. A *numeral* is a number, to *enumerate* is to list, and *supernumeraries* are extra people.

ACR means sharp. An *acrid* smell such as that of ammonia is sharp, *acerbity* is sharpness of temper, and *acrimony* is a sharp and heated dispute.

REVIEW STEMS FROM *CAESAR'S ENGLISH I*

stem	meaning	modern examples
ject	throw	subject, dejected, interjection
dorm	sleep	dormancy, dormitive, dormient
magn	great	Magna Carta, magnum opus, magnanimous
ver	true	aver, verisimilitude, verdical
put	think	impute, computer, dispute

cant acrimonious patricide exculpate
ition numeracy depopulate matricide
on fusion culpable vitamin transform
pugnant urban patrilineal comprador
patronize video transitive commence
rimony enumerate germinal compost
difuse segregate oppugn paternalism
migrate abrupt commix combinative
occlude plurality acrid urbanologist
rate transoceanic suffuse ingratitude
uitious urbanize germicide segregate
pulace matrilocal vitalize matrilineal
mistranslate numeral patronage vide
migrate inculpate repatriated seduce
tor transgression evidence disruptive
lude select nonplussed alphanumeric
rate expatriated urbanity pugnacious
ratulate preclude transfusion grateful
videlicet culprit migratory numerous
secede suburb numerology secession

NONFICTION WORDS

Here are five important nonfiction words. You might not hear them often in daily conversation, but you will encounter them frequently in your future academic life. Each word is based on one of the stems in the lesson.

stem	word	definition
culp	**exculpate**	to free from blame
pugn	**impugn**	to dispute the truth
urb	**urbane**	refined
numer	**enumerate**	to list
acr	**acrimony**	bitterness

EXCULPATE is a verb that means to free from blame, to declare innocent. The noun form is *exculpation*. In Sir Walter Scott's *Ivanhoe*, we read that "Gurth, knowing his master's irritable temper, attempted no exculpation."

IMPUGN, pronounced im-PYOON, is a verb that means to dispute the truth of a statement, to call a statement into question. You can impugn someone's testimony. In *Ivanhoe*, Sir Walter Scott wrote of "those who impugn our authority."

URBANE is an adjective that means suave, courteous, refined, cosmopolitan in manner. The noun form is *urbanity*. In Henry James's *The American*, we read, "he was determined to seem even more urbane than usual."

ENUMERATE is a verb that means to list, to mention things one by one. In his *Autobiography*, Benjamin Franklin mentioned "several points of complaint which I enumerated."

ACRIMONY is a noun that refers to bitterness, hard feelings. The adjective form is *acrimonious*. In Nathaniel Hawthorne's novel *The House of the Seven Gables*, we read that "her responses were little short of acrimonious."

Write two good sentences for each word.

IMPUGN

CAESAR'S ANALOGIES: Find the most similar pairs.

PUGILIST : PUGNACIOUS ::
  a. urban : suburban
  b. culprit : culpable
  c. exculpate : innocent
  d. enumerate : items

OPPUGN : SANCTION ::
  a. pugilist : glove
  b. city : suburb
  c. supernumerary : extra
  d. exculpate : convict
  (In this question, *sanction* is a verb.)

CAESAR'S ANTONYMS: Find the best opposite.

ACRIMONY
  a. pugnacity
  b. verisimilitude
  c. urbanity
  d. harmony

PUGNACIOUS
  a. mollifying
  b. oppugning
  c. enumerating
  d. exculpating

CAESAR'S CONTEXT: Find the best word to complete the sentence.

The gladiators were trained as expert _____.
  a. culprits
  b. pugilists
  c. supernumeraries
  d. interlocutors

Prisoners captured in Gaul were rarely _____.
  a. exculpated
  b. oppugned
  c. disputed
  d. enumerated

The spectacles in the Colosseum required a great many _____.
  a. acrimonies
  b. numerals
  c. exculpations
  d. supernumeraries

CAESAR'S MATHEMATICS

CDXIX pugnacious pugilists impugned the veracity of a poet. CXLIII of those pugilists tired of the conversation and went home. One third of those who remained departed, making equivocal comments about something or other. The remaining pugilists got into an acrimonious altercation, and half of them departed, enumerating the wrongs they received. XIX of those who remained vanished into the verdure. XIV were nonplussed by the entire experience and secluded themselves in a hidden valley. The pugilists who remained changed their minds, made germane apologies, and sat down. How many pugilists sat down?

CAESAR'S ESSAY

An important part of writing academic essays is focusing sharply on the topic. If you are writing about Alexander the Great, you want your reader to be thinking about Alexander and only Alexander. That is why we avoid words that would break the spell and take the reader's mind off Alexander. We avoid first person, eliminating all references to ourselves. We avoid second person, eliminating any reference to the reader as "you." We avoid all references to the parts of the essay itself, such as the conclusion. We avoid calling quotations quotations; instead of saying "Johnson agreed, as in the following quotation where he states...," we can just say Johnson agreed, creating a smooth and undistracting transition:

> Those who felt wronged in the dispute claimed that they had been misunderstood and misrepresented. Johnson agreed, saying that "There was never so much injustice in the state as when the James company closed the factory."

Write a short essay, practicing the avoidance of all first person and all self-reference.

CAESAR'S WORD SEARCH

In the puzzle, find the Latin-based English words that you see below. They might be vertical, horizontal, or diagonal. Always notice the stems that are in the words.

Y	R	F	P	U	D	E	S	S	U	L	P	N	O	N
Q	W	E	A	O	D	S	E	C	L	U	D	E	N	R
E	R	X	Y	G	L	S	K	K	C	E	K	J	G	U
Y	F	C	R	T	Y	N	O	M	I	C	R	A	E	R
T	G	U	A	E	N	A	F	O	R	P	H	M	R	B
I	H	L	R	V	T	X	O	D	O	H	T	R	O	A
B	J	P	E	Q	U	I	V	O	C	A	L	A	U	N
R	K	A	M	I	Y	H	O	G	E	R	M	A	N	E
E	L	T	U	C	U	L	P	A	B	L	E	R	C	E
C	U	E	N	U	P	U	G	N	A	C	I	O	U	S
A	R	C	R	S	U	E	R	U	D	R	E	V	M	N
A	B	X	E	T	A	R	E	M	U	N	E	V	S	P
S	A	F	P	U	I	O	A	S	I	R	O	H	L	W
E	N	G	U	P	M	I	C	U	T	U	M	U	L	T
R	Y	G	S	C	P	R	E	C	L	U	D	E	S	V

exculpate	acrimony	supernumerary	orthodox
impugn	culpable	acerbity	profane
urbane	pugnacious	verdure	tumult
enumerate	urban	equivocal	preclude
seclude	nonplussed	germane	

1. Which of these words is the most interesting?
2. Which of these words will you use most often?
3. Which two words are related to each other in some way?
4. Which word sounds most scholarly or academic?
5. Which word has the most precise meaning?

CAESAR'S CLASSIC WORDS CHALLENGE

If we want to get a feel for how words are used, we must see how great writers use words. In each case below, one of the choices was the word used by the author. For you, this is a word game. Your challenge is to guess which word the author used. This is not a test; it is a game because more than one word choice may work perfectly well. See if you can use your sensitivity and intuition to guess which word the author used. You may need a dictionary.

1. From Frederick Douglass's *Narrative*

   I would allow myself to suffer...rather than _____ myself.
   - a. enumerate
   - b. oppugn
   - c. exculpate
   - d. impute

2. From James Watson's *The Double Helix*

   Rosy and Gosling were _____ assertive.
   - a. urbanely
   - b. acrimoniously
   - c. culpably
   - d. pugnaciously

3. From Charlotte Brontë's *Jane Eyre*

   [They treated] her with coldness and _____.
   - a. enumeration
   - b. acrimony
   - c. pugnacity
   - d. urbanity

CAESAR'S GRAMMAR · PHRASES

The first three sentences below are worked out for you. See if you can solve the next four, identifying the parts of speech, parts of sentence, and phrases for each sentence. Remember, if you see an *-ing* word, it might be a verb, or a gerund, or a participle. You have to notice what it is doing in the sentence.

1. **Impugning** his report, the general gave Nero a warning.
   adj.   adj.   n.   adj.   n.   v.   n.   adj.   n.
                         subj.   AVP   I.O.   D.O.
   -----------participial phrase-----------

2. **Enumerating** the wrongdoings was a **doleful** task.
       n.   adj.   n.   v.   adj.   adj.   n.
   ----------------------------subj.----------------------------   LVP   S.C.
   ----------------------gerund phrase----------------------

3. The new policies avoided causing **acrimonious** altercations.
   adj.   adj.   n.   v.   n.   adj.   n.
          subj.   AVP   ----------------------------D.O.----------------------------
                         ----------------------gerund phrase----------------------

4. **Exculpating** Decius completely, the general left the tent.

5. With his **urbane** compliment, Caius pleased the hostess.

6. Ignoring Agrippa's **pugnacious** countenance, Gaius laughed aloud.

7. The invasion **precluded** making peace with the Gauls.

Here is a four-level analysis of a sentence using the adjective *pugnacious*, which means combative, ready to fight.

	The	**pugnacious**	Gauls	were	no	match	for	the	legions.
Parts of Speech:	adj.	adj.	n.	v.	adj.	n.	prep.	adj.	n.
Parts of Sentence:			subj.	LVP		S.C.			
Phrases:							--prep. phrase--		
Clauses:	one independent clause; a simple declarative sentence								

Here the adjective *pugnacious* modifies the plural noun *Gauls*. This sentence give us another great example of a subject complement; the linking verb *were* helps the subject complement *match* equate back to the subject.

One of the secrets of advanced vocabulary is knowing how to alter words in order to use them as different parts of speech. Pick one example from each column below, and write a good sentence using it.

noun	adjective	verb	adverb
enumeration	enumerated	enumerate	-
pugnacity	pugnacious	-	pugnaciously
urbanity	urbane	-	urbanely
acrimony	acrimonious	-	acrimoniously
exculpation	exculpated	exculpate	-
magnanimity	magnanimous	-	magnanimously
culpability	culpable	-	culpably
dejection	dejected	-	dejectedly

ACTIUM, 2 SEPT., 31 B.C.
Michael Clay Thompson

Actium was the turning point.
You could say that. The Roman Republic,
that 500-year audition of voices,
stopped on this day. Octavian day.

That profane fool Antony and his nonplussed Cleo,
they never had a chance. At Actium, I mean.
As Hopalong would say, they were all hat and no cattle.
Probably didn't even believe it themselves.
It's neither here nor there. It was Octavian's day.

Like a continental divide, Actium.
From here, water flows west. One foot to the right,
the water flows east. Like that.
From this battle backward, a republic,
with a big-deal Senate. From this day forward,
an Empire, led by the princeps, Augustus: Octavian.
That's the germane point. Good fight for Octavian,
Peremptory Man.

One of history's great disruptions.
Didn't take Octavian long to turn a sow's republic
into a silk Empire—if you take his view of the matter.
We could impugn his stand, you know,
declaim the ostentation of His Impassive Highness.
But he was magnanimous at times, we suppose,
and orthodox history—that torpid process—
exculpates Octavian.
Oh...Au-gus-tus. Sorry.

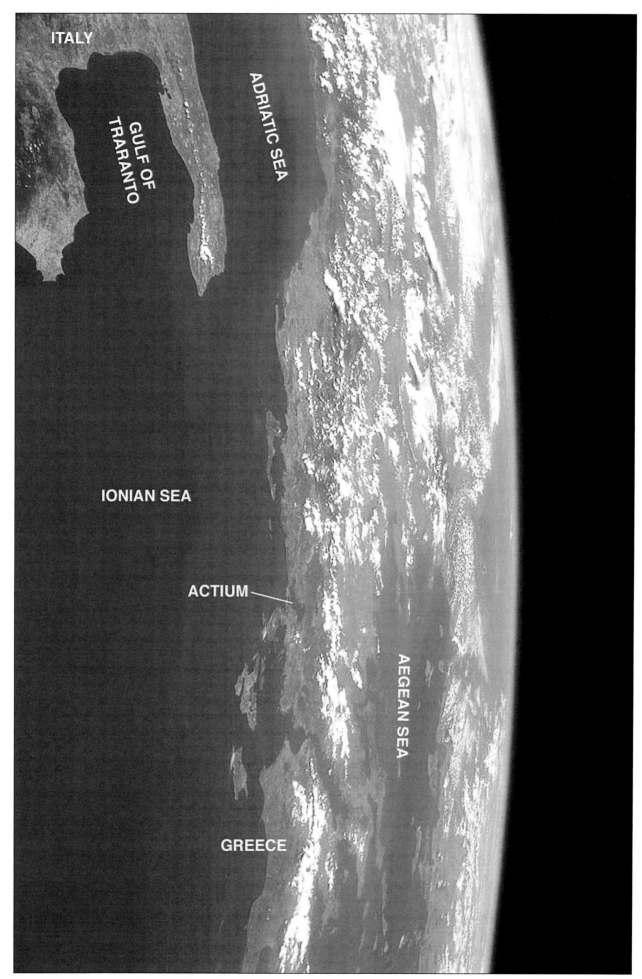

ITALY

GULF OF TRARANTO

ADRIATIC SEA

IONIAN SEA

ACTIUM

AEGEAN SEA

GREECE

ROMAN GREECE

In 27 B.C., Emperor Augustus defined Greece as the Roman province of Achaea. Most of Greece had come under Roman control when Lucius Mummius sacked Corinth in 146 B.C., with many of the islands in the Aegean Sea being added to Rome's dominion in 133 B.C.

Athens and other Greek cities attempted to revolt in 88 B.C., but the Roman general Sulla overpowered Greek resistance. Sulla constructed massive siege works around Athens and its port of Piraeus. Even in the face of impending defeat, the Athenians did not surrender, and Sulla tightened his grip on the city until the starved inhabitants were reduced to eating grass and leather. Finally the Athenians sent a somber delegation to speak with Sulla, but upon meeting with him, they did not importune him for mercy but subjected him to an acrimonious tirade about the greatness of Athens. Rather than impugn their assertions, Sulla dismissed them with a derisive retort: "I was sent to Athens, not to take lessons, but to reduce rebels to obedience." Sulla assigned his engineers to undermine a large section of the Athenian defensive walls, and after the wall collapsed, the Romans conducted a sublunary midnight sack of the great city. When the sanguinary battle was over, Athens was prostrate, and the port of Piraeus had been burned to the ground.

The victory was purely military. An infusion of Greek mathematics, science, art, poetry, philosophy, and literature was a powerful influence on Roman civilization. The poet Horace wrote that "*Graecia capta ferum victorem cepit*": Captive Greece captured her rude conqueror. Virgil imitated Homer's epics in his *Aeneid*. Romans made beautiful copies of Greek sculpture to decorate their homes and public buildings. They imitated Greek architecture. Once Greece was under Roman control, many emperors built important buildings in Greek cities, especially in Athens. Hadrian ordered the construction of an important arch, the Arch of Hadrian, in Athens. In 66 A.D. Emperor Nero went to Greece and competed in the Olympic Games.

Greece was subject to many of the same invasions that the rest of the Roman Empire suffered. Before Alaric and his Visigoths invaded Italy and sacked Rome in 410 A.D., they invaded Greece and sacked Athens.

Greece eventually formed part of the Byzantine Empire and became Christianized under Constantine's benevolent reign, laying the foundation for the Orthodox Greek Church.

THRACE

BYZANTIUM

MACEDON

THESSALONICA

HELLESPONT

MT OLYMPUS

TROY

THESSALY

AEGEAN
SEA

DELPHI

THEBES

GREECE

CORINTH

ATHENS

MYCENAE

SPARTA

SEA OF CRETE

RHODES

CRETE

OVID'S STORIES OF THE ROMAN PANTHEON

When we read the Roman myths, we often read a modern book that not only translates the myths into English but also smooths out some of the more profane or sensual details found in the frank Roman versions of the stories. But where do those modern writers get the stories? The primary ancient source for Roman myths is the *Metamorphoses*, by Publius Ovidius Naso, whom we know as Ovid, pronounced AH-vid, rhyming roughly with *Hobbit*. Together with Virgil and Horace, Ovid is regarded as one of the three great poets of Roman literature and has been a major influence on authors such as Shakespeare and Dante, as well as numerous painters and sculptors such as Bernini.

Ovid was born in Sulmo, a town east of Rome, in 43 B.C. and lived until 18 A.D. His father wished him to study law, but after an initial attempt to follow his father's wishes, he discontinued law and devoted himself to becoming a poet, to his father's profound disappointment. Ovid's talent propelled him to Rome's attention, and he became a favorite of literary circles for twenty-five years. Eventually he angered Emperor Augustus, and in 8 A.D., for reasons not entirely clear, Augustus exiled Ovid to Tomis, a city on the Black Sea, far from Rome. Ovid's life in exile was sad and isolated; he had no access to libraries or to the urbane excitement of Rome. He even wrote a book titled *Tristia*—sadness—to capture the lonely ignominy of his existence. He lived only ten more years.

Ovid's magnum opus, the *Metamorphoses*, is a collection of 250 myths of the Roman pantheon, the community of gods. Ovid chose the title *Metamorphoses* to feature the transformation (*meta*) in shape (*morph*) that typically occurs in the myths, as from a human being to a bird, or from a human being to a tree. In the myth of Daphne and Apollo, for example, Apollo chases the beautiful Daphne through the forest until he catches her, at which point she changes into a tree, her feet shooting roots down into the ground and her hands and hair bursting into leaves. The great Italian sculptor Gian Lorenzo Bernini created a masterpiece depicting the moment of Daphne's metamorphosis.

IGNOMINY

Photo by Dr. Thomas Milton Kemnitz

VIRIATUS, THE TERROR OF THE ROMANS

Dr. Myriam Borges Thompson

After 200 years of resistance, the Romanization of the Iberian Peninsula was finally accomplished. This occurred only after two transcendent events: the death in 138 B.C. of Viriatus, the military leader of the Lusitanians, and the fall five years later of the Celtiberian settlement of Numantia after thirteen months of Roman siege. In an acrimonious act of defiance (see next page), the Numantians chose to burn their possessions and die free before acquiescing to Roman rule.

Historians know little about Viriatus, whose talent, bravery, and charisma elevated him to a hero of symbolic and epic proportions and who for eight years defeated every general Rome sent to fight him.

Some facts are certain: the Romans did not know Viriatus's family name. This means that Viriatus likely came from a plebeian family because all of the elite Celtiberian families were well-known to the Romans. We know also that Viriatus was a man of intellect, strength, valor, and adherence to a strict but benevolent personal code of honor. His magnanimous character caused thousands of men to follow him blindly.

Viriatus's probable plebeian background means that he was likely a shepherd, a hunter, a bandit, and then a stellar soldier who rose to power by his brilliant mind and personal attributes. What we know from Roman historians' chronicles is that Viriatus led the resistance to Rome in Hispania Citerior, the northwestern regions of today's Spain and Portugal. In a peace treaty with the Roman Senate, Viriatus was declared *amicus populi Romani*, an ally of the Roman people, after he spared the lives of Roman general Quintus Fabius Maximus Servilianus and his soldiers in the Sierra Morena mountains.

In a lurid turn of events, Viriatus was martyred when Quintus Fabius's brother, mortified by the terms of Viriatus's treaty with the Roman Senate, ordered three of Viriatus's own men to kill him in his sleep.

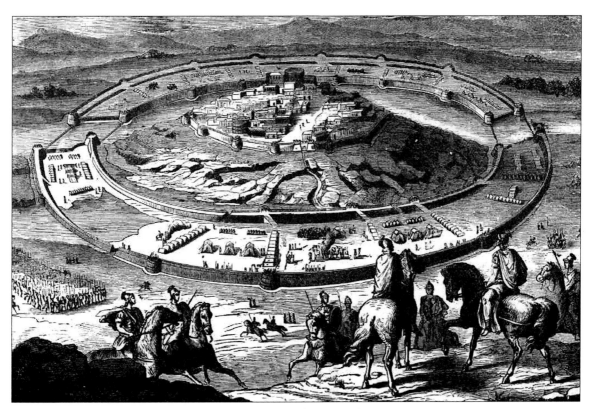

The Siege of Numantia

Viriatus was not Rome's only problem in Iberia. For more than twenty years, the Celtiberian inhabitants of Numantia resisted and often defeated the Romans, as in 137 B.C.—the year before Viriatus's death—when 20,000 Roman soldiers surrendered to 8,000 Numantians. After years of battles and the humilliation of several Roman generals, Publis Cornelius Scipio, or Scipio Africanus, the conqueror of Carthage, led more than 30,000 soldiers in the siege of Numantia. Scipio ordered the building of a stone wall system almost six miles long with 100 towers that eventually gave the Romans victory and subsequent control of the ruins of Numantia.

MORTIFY

THE ROMAN ORGANIZATION
Dr. Thomas Milton Kemnitz

The Romans were successful and powerful because they were flexible and pragmatic. During a period of four centuries when they won the battles that left them in control of Italy, they did not enslave or oppress or mortify the people they defeated. On the contrary, instead of subjecting them to gratuitous insults, they turned them into allies, gave them privileges within the Roman system, and encouraged them to find ways to cooperate rather than compete with Rome.

The result was that a huge number of people came to think of their interests as the same as Rome's. When Hannibal invaded Rome, the Romans faced their greatest antagonist ever. The risk of impending defeat hung over Rome. Hannibal was a genius with a large army of 30,000 or so, but the Roman enlistment list of men from all over Italy was said to be 700,000 strong; Rome could—and did—wear Hannibal down and outlast him. As it rose to become the dominant power, Rome lost many battles but always won the war because it always had the numerical advantage.

The Romans also learned from their adversaries. They copied successful tactics and superior weapons wherever they saw them. Fighting in Spain for the first time in about 215 B.C., they saw a helmet design they liked and subsequently copied, and they also copied their opponents' swords.

The Roman army also changed its fighting formations several times as it lost battles to better-organized enemies. The final organization of ten cohorts in a legion proved more effective than any other in the world, and it persisted for half a millenium until Rome's fall, the germane point being that Rome's fall was the result more of internal disarray than of military inadequacy.

GERMANE

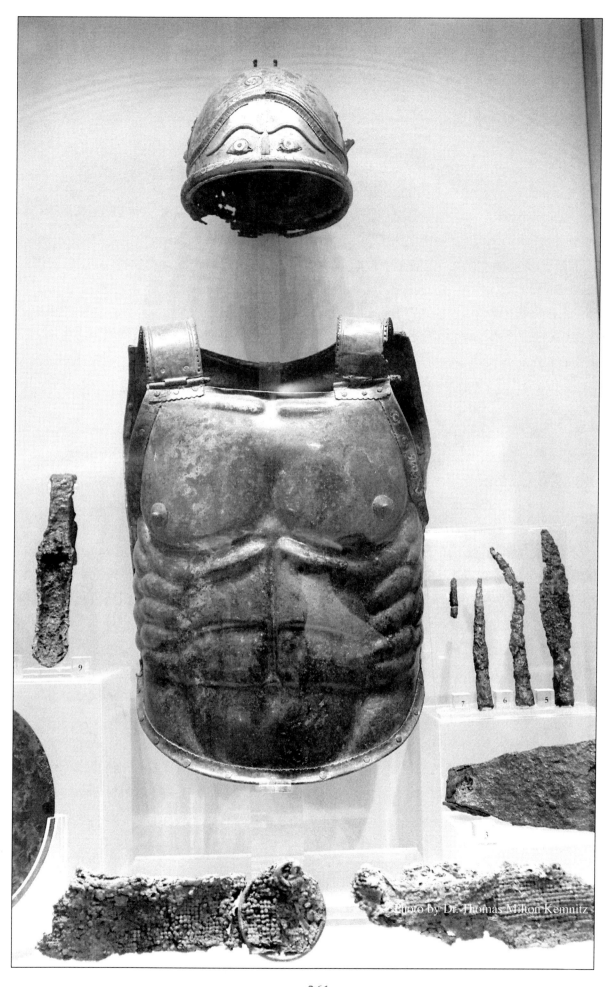

Photo by Dr. Thomas Milton Kemnitz

CAESAR AND THE END OF THE REPUBLIC
Dr. Thomas Milton Kemnitz

Julius Caesar crossed the Rubicon on the night of January 10/11, 49 B.C. It was the act that led to a long series of civil wars that ended the Roman Republic. The Romans claimed that their Republic had been founded in 509 B.C., so it was more than 460 years old when Caesar crossed the Rubicon.

The Rubicon was a small, <u>torpid</u>, muddy river in northeastern Italy that divided the province of Cisalpine Gaul from Italy; Caesar was governor of the province and allowed to have troops there, but he was not allowed to have troops in Italy itself. Once he crossed the Rubicon with his troops, Caesar became an enemy of the state. Not only was Caesar himself committing a capital offense, but so was each of his legionnaires; if captured, they were liable to be executed for treason.

Why did Caesar take such a gamble? The short but germane answer is to preclude exile: his acrimonious opponents left him with no choice except to go into seclusion for the rest of his life. His opponents were the patricians in the Senate who for the previous eighty years had killed officials who opposed them. Sometimes there were trials and then executions; other times there were simply executions or their opponents died in fights in the streets. If Caesar returned without his army, the senators planned to try and either execute or banish him. Some office holders such as Mark Antony supported Caesar, but threats from the Senate had sent them running for their lives.

The senators did not compromise with Caesar and were unwilling to share power with him because they and their predecessors had a long history of getting their way. They counted on Pompey the Great to protect them from Caesar's legions; when he could not, many of them accepted pardons from Caesar only to turn around three or four years later and do as their ancestors had done—kill their opponent. This time, however, they lost control of events, and the Republic, which had served their class so well, was doomed to tumultuous civil war.

ACRIMONY

Photo by Dr. Thomas Milton Kemnitz

REVIEW FOR CUMULATIVE QUIZ

com	together	**vita**	life	**intra**	within
vid	look	**cent**	one hundred	**pater**	father
ad	to	**matri**	mother	**fer**	carry
pop	people	**loco**	place	**sur**	over
alter	other	**contra**	against	**stell**	star
amat	love	**luna**	moon	**greg**	group
clam	cry out	**tang**	touch	**mar**	sea
junct	join	**luc**	light	**medi**	middle
tempor	time	**grat**	pleasing	**curr**	run
trans	across	**migr**	wander	**rupt**	break
clud	close	**se**	apart	**plu**	more
germ	vital	**fus**	pour	**culp**	blame
pugn	fight	**urb**	city	**numer**	number
acr	sharp				

placate	to appease	**commandeer**	officially take control
derision	ridicule	**intramural**	within an institution
vivacious	full of life	**centennial**	of a 100th anniversary
procure	to acquire	*ad infinitum*	again and again forever
retort	a quick, clever reply	**infer**	conclude from evidence
vitality	strength, energy	**audible**	able to be heard
videlicet (viz.)	namely	**benevolent**	charitable
paternal	of the father	**somber**	gloomy
matriarch	female head of family	**prostrate**	lying flat
populous	densely populated	**profuse**	abundant
localized	restricted to a place	**surfeit**	an excessive amount
altercation	a noisy argument	**contrary**	the opposite
stellar	of a star	**ostentatious**	showy
inexorable	inevitable	**indolent**	lazy
doleful	mournful	**alacrity**	eagerness
amatory	romantic	**sublunar**	under the moon
aggregate	a collected mass	**declaim**	speak against
entangled	snared, involved	**oblique**	indirect or slanting
pensive	thoughtful	**magnanimous**	generous
importune	to pester	**peremptory**	dictatorial
mariner	a sailor	**adjunct**	an unessential addition
elucidate	to explain	**mediate**	to intervene
temporize	to delay	**tacit**	unspoken
affable	friendly	**sanguine**	cheerfully confident
torpid	sluggish	**mortify**	profoundly humiliate
gratuitous	uncalled for	**concur**	to agree
transcend	to go beyond limits	**migratory**	moving seasonally
disruption	a disturbing interruption	**obsequious**	cringing, submissive
ignominy	disgrace	**acquiescence**	passive compliance
impassive	expressionless, without emotion	**impending**	about to happen
preclude	prevent	**seclude**	isolate from people
nonplussed	confused	**germane**	relevant
infusion	an inpouring	**verdure**	vegetation
equivocal	ambiguous	**orthodox**	traditional
profane	irreverent	**tumult**	disturbance
exculpate	to free from blame	**impugn**	to dispute the truth
urbane	refined	**enumerate**	to list
acrimony	bitterness		

Hasten slowly.

- Augustus

LESSON XVI · CLASSIC WORDS

English	Spanish
incongruous: incompatible	*incongruo*
malevolence: ill will	*malevolencia*
ambiguous: uncertain	*ambiguo*
felicity: great happiness	*felicidad*
irrevocable: unalterable	*irrevocable*

INCONGRUOUS (in-KON-gru-us)

The English adjective *incongruous*, from the Latin *incongruus*, means incompatible, lacking congruity. Things are incongruous when they do not go together. John F. Kennedy wrote of "this unmanageable mass of incongruous bills, each an impediment to the other" in *Profiles in Courage*. In *The War of the Worlds*, H.G. Wells wrote that "the trouble was the blank incongruity of this serenity and the swift death flying yonder." Thomas Hardy wrote in *The Return of the Native* that "The incongruity between the men's deeds and their environment was great." Robert Louis Stevenson wrote in *Treasure Island* that it "was all held together by a system of the most various and incongruous fastenings, brass buttons, bits of stick, and loops of tarry gaskin." In Charles Dickens's *Great Expectations*, there are "sparely-furnished chambers with incongruous upholstery work." Jane Austen, in *Emma*, described "the seeming incongruity of gentle manners and a conceited head." Why are gentle manners and a conceited head incongruous?

MALEVOLENCE (mal-LEV-o-lence)

Malevolence, from the Latin *malevolens*, is ill (*mal*) will (*vol*); it is an evil intention to do harm. In Harper Lee's *To Kill a Mockingbird*, we read that "Inside the house lived a malevolent phantom." In Joseph Heller's *Catch-22,* there is "a hatchet-faced man with sunken acrimonious eyes and a thin, malevolent mouth." James Baldwin wrote in *Go Tell It on the Mountain* that "his eyes were so wild and depthlessly malevolent, and his mouth was twisted into such a snarl of pain." Bernard Malamud, in *The Natural*, wrote that "he saw Mercy in a nearby seat, gazing at him with a malevolent sneer." In *White Fang,* Jack London wrote that White Fang "snarled and bristled and glared malevolently." And in Emily Brontë's *Wuthering Heights*, we read, "What malevolence you must have to wish to convince me that there is no happiness in the world."

AMBIGUOUS (am-BIG-yoo-us)

Our English adjective *ambiguous* (the noun is *ambiguity*) comes from the Latin *ambiguus* and refers to the kind of uncertainty we feel when there are multiple possible meanings, and we are not sure which one is meant. Conversely, a clear meaning is *unambiguous*. In *Invisible Man*, Ralph Ellison wrote that there was "another ambiguity to puzzle my groping mind: Why is a bird-soiled statue more commanding than one that is clean?" Robert Penn Warren wrote in *All the King's Men* that "I could detect a curious shifting and shading of feelings on her face, too evanescent and ambiguous for definition." In Thomas Hardy's *The Mayor of Casterbridge*, a character is "looking round upon the idlers with that ambiguous gaze of his, which at one moment seemed to mean satisfaction, and at another fiery disdain." And in Shakespeare's *Romeo and Juliet*, we see the request to "Seal up the mouth of outrage for a while, 'til we can clear these ambiguities."

FELICITY (feh-LISS-ih-tee)

The English noun *felicity* comes from the Latin *felix*, happy. The adjective form is *felicitous*. Felicity is great happiness. In Rudyard Kipling's novel *Kim*, written in 1901, "they enjoyed themselves in high felicity." In *Moby Dick*, Melville wrote that "even the highest earthly felicities ever have a certain unsignifying pettiness lurking in them." Charles Dickens, in *A Tale of Two Cities*, described Miss Pross, "whose eyes were red with felicity." Jane Austen used *felicity* in *Emma*: "What felicity it is to hear a tune again which has made one happy." Mark Twain gives us one of the most surprising uses of *felicity*; in *Tom Sawyer*, Twain wrote that "it mightily increased his dismal felicity." Whatever can Twain have meant by that? One of the clearest uses of *felicity* comes from Benjamin Franklin's *Autobiography*: "I grew convinced," Franklin wrote, "that truth, sincerity, and integrity in dealings between man and man were of the utmost importance to the felicity of life."

IRREVOCABLE (ir-re-VOKE-uh-bul)

The English adjective *irrevocable* comes from the Latin *irrevocabilis* and refers to something that cannot (*ir*) be called (*voc*) back (*re*)—that cannot be revoked. In *Song of Solomon*, Nobel Prize-winner Toni Morrison wrote that "There was no real anger and nothing irrevocable was said." Marjorie Kennan Rawlings wrote in *The Yearling* that "He braced himself against the frenzy to which he was irrevocably attached." In *A Portrait of the Artist as a Young Man*,

James Joyce wrote that "a definite and irrevocable act of his threatened to end for ever, in time and in eternity, his freedom." Herman Melville wrote in *Moby Dick* that "it is always as well to have a look at him before irrevocably committing yourself into his hands." In Mary Shelley's *Frankenstein*, we read, "Listen to my history, and you will perceive how irrevocably it is determined." More than four centuries ago, Shakespeare wrote in *As You Like It*: "Firm and irrevocable is my doom." What do you think Toni Morrison meant by nothing irrevocable being said?

REVIEW WORDS FROM *CAESAR'S ENGLISH I*

articulate: express clearly
vex: to irritate
prostrate: lying down
abyss: bottomless depth
martyr: one who suffers

CAESAR'S MATHEMATICS

CLXXIII malevolent centurions made irrevocable comments about the emperor. The emperor declared LXXV of the centurions' comments ambiguous and asked for clarification. The other centurions felt a sense of felicity not to have been asked, but then the emperor declared their comments acrimonious and asked that half of them leave. The other half thought that they had been exculpated, but suddenly the emperor asked XXVI of them to endorse orthodox imperial ideas or be troubled with an unpleasant assignment, and the frightened centurions fell over, unconscious. The emperor than praised the remaining centurions for their sagacity. How many centurions did he praise?

FELICITY

CAESAR'S WORD SEARCH

In the puzzle, find the Latin-based English words that you see below. They might be vertical, horizontal, or diagonal. Always notice the stems that are in the words.

U	E	R	A	E	T	A	P	L	U	C	X	E	T	Y
N	N	P	E	N	A	B	R	U	L	P	L	V	T	E
S	U	R	Q	A	T	K	R	E	V	B	I	I	R	D
U	M	E	B	F	P	A	T	L	A	O	C	Y	M	L
O	E	C	B	O	R	T	E	C	J	I	X	T	A	H
U	R	L	I	R	E	X	O	R	L	O	U	C	L	D
G	A	U	M	P	X	V	K	E	D	F	O	E	E	E
I	T	D	A	P	E	M	F	O	H	V	I	D	V	S
B	E	E	N	R	G	U	H	F	I	M	T	U	O	S
M	X	E	R	A	C	T	M	U	P	G	L	L	L	U
A	M	I	E	S	R	J	Q	U	E	D	U	C	E	L
M	A	I	L	O	X	E	G	W	S	D	M	E	N	P
I	S	I	N	C	O	N	G	R	U	O	U	S	C	N
A	C	R	I	M	O	N	Y	T	W	F	T	H	E	O
C	E	R	U	D	R	E	V	H	X	U	R	B	A	N

incongruous	exculpate	verdure	tumult
malevolence	impugn	equivocal	preclude
ambiguous	urbane	orthodox	seclude
felicity	enumerate	profane	nonplussed
irrevocable	acrimony	urban	

1. Which of these words has the most beautiful sound?
2. Which of these words will you see in novels?
3. Which word is most unusual?
4. Which word is the most scholarly or academic?
5. Which word has the most exact meaning?

CAESAR'S CLASSIC WORDS CHALLENGE

If we want to get a feel for how words are used, we must see how great writers use words. In each case below, one of the choices was the word used by the author. For you, this is a word game. Your challenge is to guess which word the author used. This is not a test; it is a game because more than one word choice may work perfectly well. See if you can use your sensitivity and intuition to guess which word the author used. You may need a dictionary.

1. From James Baldwin's *Go Tell It on the Mountain*

   [The cat] turned to watch them, with yellow, _____ eyes.
   - a. malevolent
   - b. ambiguous
   - c. incongruous
   - d. irrevocable

2. From Robert Penn Warren's *All the King's Men*

   It was a(n) _____, speculative look.
   - a. malevolent
   - b. ambiguous
   - c. irrevocable
   - d. felicitous

3. From Jane Austen's *Pride and Prejudice*

   They were one of those _____ and impossible married couples.
   - a. ambiguous
   - b. irrevocable
   - c. incongruous
   - d. malevolent

CAESAR'S GRAMMAR · CLAUSES

In the first fifteen lessons, we explored vocabulary in terms of the grammar that displays its usage. We looked at parts of speech, parts of sentence, and phrases. A word might, for example, be a noun and also a subject, or a noun and also an object of preposition. By thinking of vocabulary this way, we can see what the word is doing in the sentence.

There is a fourth level of grammar for us to examine, and that is **clauses**. In a way we already understand clauses because a clause is simply *a group of words that contains a subject and its predicate*. The clause is the subject, the predicate, and all of the words that go with it. For example, we might write:

The **Romans prepared** well, and **they responded** quickly.
----------------independent clause---------------   ------------independent clause----------

In this sentence, there are two clauses. The first clause is "The Romans prepared well," and the second clause is "they responded quickly." Notice that each clause has its own subject and verb. In this example the coordinating conjunction *and* that joins the two clauses is not part of either clause; it is only glue. An **independent** clause makes sense by itself: *Caesar refused to bargain*, and a **dependent clause** does not make sense by itself: *when the Gauls arrived at his camp*. So a sentence can have an independent clause with a dependent clause attached to it:

Caesar refused to bargain when the **Gauls arrived** at his camp.
--------------independent clause------------   ---------------------dependent clause------------------------

All of this reminds us that words are not dead; they do things. Every vocabulary word is busy doing something important.

In order to understand clauses well, we must know the difference between the coordinating conjunctions (*and*, *but*, *or*, *nor*, *for*, *so*, *yet*) and the subordinating conjunctions (*if*, *as*, *since*, *when*, *because*, and many others). Coordinating conjunctions join two independent clauses together into a **compound sentence**, but subordinating conjunctions often begin dependent clauses and join the dependent clause to an independent clause to make a **complex sentence**. In a complex sentence, the dependent clause can be either first or second.

Compound sentence (two independent clauses):

Caesar moved his legions at once, but **Vercingetorix escaped**.
--------------------independent clause--------------------   ----------independent clause----------

Complex sentences (one independent, one dependent):

The **Gauls retreated** when **Caesar invaded** their homeland.
---------independent clause------- ----------------------dependent clause------------------------

Because **Caesar hesitated**, the **Gauls escaped** into the hills.
----------------dependent clause------------- -----------------independent clause-------------------

Notice that the dependent clauses are in fact dependent. They do not make sense by themselves, and they must be attached to an independent clause. Notice also that phrases are inside clauses; every phrase is part of a clause.

The sentences that we have analyzed in the first fifteen lessons have all been one-clause sentences. We will now look at sentences that have two clauses.

Now that we include clauses, we can do four-level analysis—the method used in the *Grammar Voyage* text. We will add a clause line to the three lines of analysis that we already know. We also will use a code to describe our sentences: *I* will mean independent, *D* will mean dependent, and *cc* will mean coordinating conjunction. Can you analyze the last five sentences?

1.   **Vexing**   them,   Caesar   refused,   and   they   departed   angrily.
        adj.   pron.   n.   v.   conj.   pron.   v.   adv.
                               subj.   AVP   subj.   AVP
    -----participial phrase----
    ----------------------independent clause-------------------   -----------independent clause-----------
    Note: This is a compound sentence containing two independent clauses: I,ccI.

2.   As   Caesar   invaded   Gaul,   **traversing**   the   forest   slowed   the   legion.
    conj.   n.   v.   n.   n.   adj.   n.   v.   adj.   n.
             subj.   AVP   D.O.   ---------------- subj.-----------------   AVP   D.O.
                                       -----------gerund phrase-----------
    -----------------dependent clause-------------   --------------------------independent clause------------------------
    Note: This is a complex sentence with the dependent clause first: D,I.

3.

Caesar	was	**vexed**	when	his	generals	arrived	at	the	tent.
n.	v.	adj.	conj.	adj.	n.	v.	prep.	adj.	n.
subj.	LVP	S.C.			subj.	AVP			

----prep. phrase-----

--------------independent clause---------- -------------------------dependent clause---------------------------

Note: This is an ID complex sentence. We do not use a comma to separate the clauses in an ID structure.

4. **Vexing** Caesar, Brutus objected as the debate began.

independent *.dependent*
clauses *clauses*

5. Because he was **malevolent**, Cassius gave Brutus a look.

dependent *independent*
clauses *clauses*

6. The order was **irrevocable** because his legions invaded.

independent *dependent?*
clauses

7. Invading Carthage was risky if the **incongruous** omen was true.

independent *dependent*
clauses

8. Because he was **articulate**, he enjoyed hearing himself.

dependent *independent*
clauses

Here is a four-level analysis of a sentence using the adjective *ambiguous*, which means uncertain.

	Caesar's	order	was	not	**ambiguous**;	it	was	clear.
Parts of Speech:	n.	n.	v.	adv.	adj.	pron.	v.	adj.
Parts of Sentence:		subj.	LVP		S.C.	subj.	LVP	S.C.
Phrases:	no prepositional, appositive, or verbal phrases							
Clauses:	---------------independent clause------------- an I;I compound declarative sentence				-indep. clause-			

Here is a nice compound sentence. Because there is no conjunction joining the two independent clauses, we use a semicolon between the clauses: I;I. Each clause contains a linking verb followed by a subject complement. The adjective *ambiguous* modifies the noun *order*.

One of the secrets of advanced vocabulary is knowing how to alter words in order to use them as different parts of speech. Pick one example from each column below, and write a good sentence using it.

noun	adjective	verb	adverb
equivocation	equivocal	equivocate	equivocally
orthodoxy	orthodox	-	-
tumult	tumultuous	-	tumultuously
profanity	profane	profane	profanely
sagacity	sagacious	-	sagaciously
wistfulness	wistful	-	wistfully

CAESAR'S SESQUIPEDALIAN STORY

An orthodox strategy would be to camp on the plain, construct defenses, and draw the odious Gauls out into the open, away from the dense verdure, but Caesar's subtle sagacity prohibited anything so tedious and irrevocable. No, with an acute intelligence almost malevolent, he sat, pensively, perplexed, working out the alternatives in his profound mind. He made no ostentatious show of his struggle, but the soldiers knew to leave him alone. Their countenances manifested confidence in Caesar; they had learned to venerate him for his singular military genius, and they were sanguine as he pondered. They traversed by him in tacit admiration and would acquiesce in any attack he planned, not because they were obsequious, but because he won. Always, Caesar won. It was as though he could see the future and always knew what was impending. The incredulous and mortified enemy always found out, too late, that with surreal insight Caesar had anticipated what they would do, and their best ideas only seemed to place them inexorably in Caesar's grip. Soon Caesar would issue his peremptory commands, and no one, not even officers, would protest against the plan because Caesar had gazed into his internal abyss and discovered a truth visible only to himself.

Once he had the solution, he was placid; his impassive visage manifested a profound serenity. He would seek some repose in the early hours of the night. At dawn, the enemy would be in for a prodigious surprise, an implacable attack that would not abate until the Romans controlled the field, and then Caesar would be magnanimous in victory as the prostrate Gauls grotesquely importuned him to spare their lives. After all, the Gauls did not want to be martyrs any more than the Romans did. And often, Caesar met their doleful pleas with an affable but condescending altruism.

An incongruous sense of benevolent felicity spread over the battlefield as everyone fell asleep except the sentries, and over the undulating hills to the east, the first pallid hints of day painted a wistful ambiguity on the low clouds. Now would come a tumult that would shatter the torpor of the night, send some running in ignominious defeat, vex the surrounding communities, and turn the derisive retorts of the Gauls into profuse expressions of gratitude that they were fortunate enough to be conquered by the Romans.

Photo by Dr. Thomas Milton Kemnitz

ARAUSIO, 6 OCT., 105 B.C.

Michael Clay Thompson

Long trudge through Gaul. That's what.
Boiorix thought back over the migration
from freezing Jutland, the Great Trek south
for warmer weather, greener fields.
This relocation irrevocable. A done deal.
No ambiguity. No going back.
Tramp tramp.

He'd led his Cimbri toughs from Jutland,
fought malevolent Germans, obsequious Gauls—
and the vexing Romans. Always Romans.
Those little warm-weather troops
in their fixed formations. Hut hut.

Organized—he'd give 'em that.
No biggy for his boys though.
His Cimbri were rough. Cold-weather guys.
Those weasel Romans better step aside.
That's how Boiorix saw it.
The Roman warrior reputation incongruous
with their iffy performance in battle.
Ha ha.

If he could ever catch those Romans together,
in some big field, he'd settle this thing. Felicity.
Send some legions to Pluto's martyr-abyss.
Leave 'em prostrate—permanently.
Just past those hills, he'd heard, is Arausio.
Get supplies there. Stock up. And scouts said
there were Romans in the region.
Good...good.

GAUL

Bay of
Biscay

Arausio

HISPANIA

At the Battle of Arausio in southern Gaul, the Cimbri, migrating south from Jutland, killed 120,000 Roman and allied soldiers—the worst loss in Roman military history.

THE CIMBRI AND JUTLAND

The Cimbri were a fierce Germanic tribe from the Jutland region of what we now call Denmark. With unambiguous intentions, the Cimbri left their cold homeland and migrated south from Jutland into Germania and Gaul (France), joining at times with the Teutones and the Ambrones to fight the Romans. The Cimbri had defeated the vexing Romans in a number of small battles, but at the Battle of Arausio in southern Gaul, the Cimbri, under the leadership of the articulate Boiorix, destroyed an enormous army of 80,000 Romans and 40,000 allies, killing everyone and inflicting the worst defeat in Roman military history. The Roman legions were divided into two groups under the mutually malevolent leadership of Quintus Servilius Caepio and Gnaeus Malius Maximus. Boiorix exploited the divided Roman leadership in his attack. The worst previous defeat had been Hannibal's defeat of Roman armies at Cannae in 216 B.C., where there had been 75,000 Roman casualties. After the Battle of Arausio, the Cimbri continued their migration, invading farther into Gaul and even into Hispania, but eventually the Romans prepared new armies and almost completely annihilated the Cimbri, who never again became a major force.

Historically, Jutland was called Cimbria. It is a large peninsula that extends into the sea toward Scandinavia. The island of Zealand, which is the location of the modern Danish capital Copenhagen, is part of Denmark.

In 1916 during World War I, the British and Germans fought one of history's greatest naval battles in the North Sea west of Jutland. The outcome was somewhat ambiguous; both sides claimed to have won, but the British lost more ships and lives, with fourteen British ships sinking to Germany's eleven. The Germans were unsuccessful in destroying the British navy and eventually resorted to submarine warfare, and between 1916 and 1917 the German U-boats sent 1.4 million tons of shipping and martyred mariners into the abyss. When they sank three American vessels, the U.S. declared war on Germany and entered the war.

AMBIGUOUS

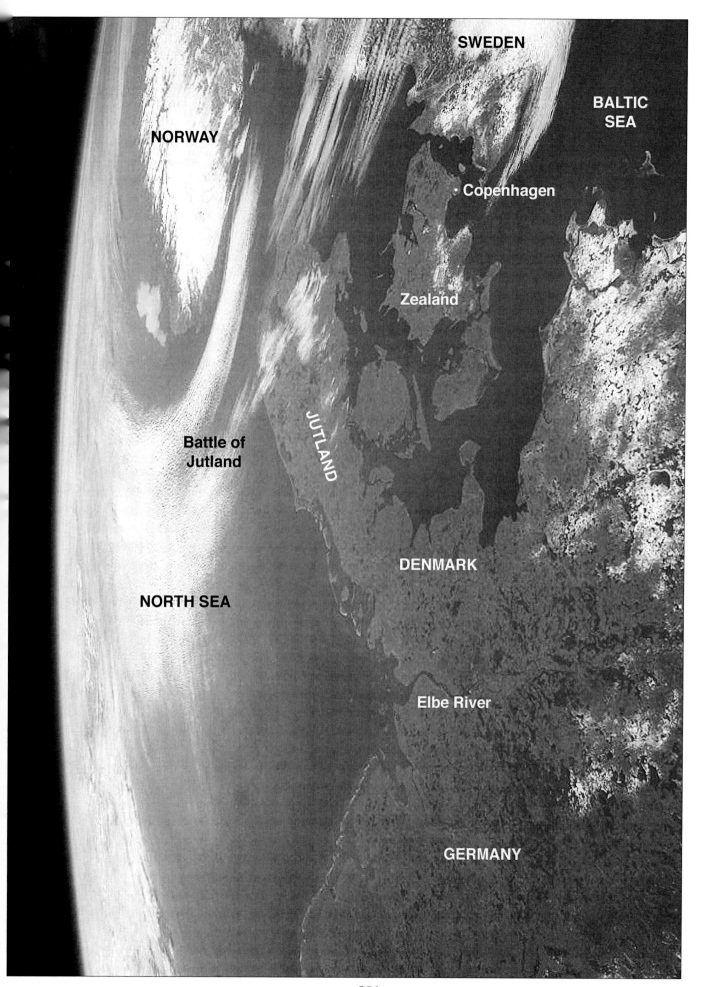

SWEDEN

BALTIC
SEA

NORWAY

• Copenhagen

Zealand

Battle of
Jutland

JUTLAND

DENMARK

NORTH SEA

Elbe River

GERMANY

REVIEW FOR CUMULATIVE QUIZ

com	together	vita	life	intra	within
vid	look	cent	one hundred	pater	father
ad	to	matri	mother	fer	carry
pop	people	loco	place	sur	over
alter	other	contra	against	stell	star
amat	love	luna	moon	greg	group
clam	cry out	tang	touch	mar	sea
junct	join	luc	light	medi	middle
tempor	time	grat	pleasing	curr	run
trans	across	migr	wander	rupt	break
clud	close	se	apart	plu	more
germ	vital	fus	pour	culp	blame
pugn	fight	urb	city	numer	number
acr	sharp				

placate	to appease	commandeer	officially take control
derision	ridicule	intramural	within an institution
vivacious	full of life	centennial	of a 100th anniversary
procure	to acquire	ad infinitum	again and again forever
retort	a quick, clever reply	infer	conclude from evidence
vitality	strength, energy	audible	able to be heard
videlicet (viz.)	namely	benevolent	charitable
paternal	of the father	somber	gloomy
matriarch	female head of family	prostrate	lying flat
populous	densely populated	profuse	abundant
localized	restricted to a place	surfeit	an excessive amount
altercation	a noisy argument	contrary	the opposite
stellar	of a star	ostentatious	showy
inexorable	inevitable	indolent	lazy
doleful	mournful	alacrity	eagerness
amatory	romantic	sublunar	under the moon
aggregate	a collected mass	declaim	speak against
entangled	snared, involved	oblique	indirect or slanting
pensive	thoughtful	magnanimous	generous
importune	to pester	peremptory	dictatorial
mariner	a sailor	adjunct	an unessential addition
elucidate	to explain	mediate	to intervene
temporize	to delay	tacit	unspoken
affable	friendly	sanguine	cheerfully confident
torpid	sluggish	mortify	profoundly humiliate
gratuitous	uncalled for	concur	to agree
transcend	to go beyond limits	migratory	moving seasonally
disruption	a disturbing interruption	obsequious	cringing, submissive
ignominy	disgrace	acquiescence	passive compliance
impassive	expressionless, without emotion	impending	about to happen
preclude	prevent	seclude	isolate from people
nonplussed	confused	germane	relevant
infusion	an inpouring	verdure	vegetation
equivocal	ambiguous	orthodox	traditional
profane	irreverent	tumult	disturbance
exculpate	to free from blame	impugn	to dispute the truth
urbane	refined	enumerate	to list
acrimony	bitterness	incongruous	incompatible
malevolence	ill will	ambiguous	uncertain
felicity	great happiness	irrevocable	unalterable

Photo by Dr. Thomas Milton Kemnitz

283

Photo by Dr. Thomas Milton Kemnitz

284

LESSON XVII · LATIN STEMS

stem	meaning	modern examples	Spanish
per	through	percolate, peregrinate, perspicacity	*perspicaz*
anim	mind	animal, animadversion, magnanimous	*magnánimo*
tort	twist	torturous, tortuous, retort	*retorta*
sanct	holy	sacrosanct, sanctimonious, sanction	*sanción*
voc	voice	vocal, invocation, vociferous	*vociferante*

PER means through. To *percolate* is to bubble through, to *peregrinate* is to wander through, and *perspicacity* is brilliant insight, the ability to see through.

ANIM means mind. *Animals* have minds in a way that plants do not, *animadversion* is criticism or blame, and *magnanimous* means being generous—great-minded.

TORT means twist. Twisting is what *torture* is named for, a *tortuous* mountain road is twisting and winding, and a *retort* is a snappy reply that you twist back on someone.

SANCT means holy. A *sacrosanct* object is very holy, a *sanctimonious* attitude is when someone acts holier than thou, and a *sanction* is an approval blessing something.

VOC means voice. *Vocals* are by the voice, an *invocation* is a call for divine presence, and a loud person is *vociferous*—full of voice.

REVIEW STEMS FROM *CAESAR'S ENGLISH I*

stem	meaning	modern examples
archy*	government	matriarch, patriarch, hierarchy
bio*	life	biogenesis, exobiology, biomorphic
auto*	self	automatic, automaton, autocracy
chron*	time	chronometer, anachronism, chronic
dec*	ten	decade, decagon, decathlon

*These stems came to the Romans from the Greek language.

unicant automaton patricide anarchy

chronological depopulate matricide

on fusion culpable vitamin transform

pugnant urban patrilineal autodidact

tronize video transitive chronograph

trimony oligarchy germinal autoharp

fuse decade oppugn paternalism vital

asynchrony autocracy autochthonous

occlude plurality acrid urbanologist

onic hierarchy ingratitude gratuitious

germicide autobiography biography

lace matrilocal biometric matrilineal

mane mistranslate numeral chronicle

le transmigrate hagiarchy repatriated

merator decagon evidence gynarchy

lude biopsy patriarchy alphanumeric

migrate expatriated urbanity decimate

se congratulate octarchy transfusion

autotroph videlicet culprit migratory

culpability decagram autocrat secede

hy biogenetic autonomy numerology

NONFICTION WORDS

Here are five important nonfiction words. You might not hear them often in daily conversation, but you will encounter them frequently in your future academic life. Each word is based on one of the stems in the lesson.

stem	word	definition
per	**perspicacity**	keen insight
anim	**magnanimous**	generous
tort	**tortuous**	twisted
sanct	**sanctimonious**	self-righteous
voc	**vociferate**	argue loudly

PERSPICACITY is a noun that means shrewdness, keen insight. The idea is that you see (*spec*) through (*per*) complications. The adjective form is *perspicacious*. In *The American*, Henry James described "an eagerness which might have made a perspicacious observer smile."

MAGNANIMOUS is an adjective that means generous or sometimes forgiving. The noun form is *magnanimity*, and the adverb form is *magnanimously*. In Thomas Hardy's novel *Jude the Obscure*, we read that "He has—so magnanimously—agreed to forgive all."

TORTUOUS is an adjective that means twisted, winding. It is a different word from *torturous*, which refers to torture. In *Uncle Tom's Cabin*, Harriet Beecher Stowe described the "abrupt, tortuous windings of the Red River."

SANCTIMONIOUS is an adjective that describes someone who makes an offensive display of being morally superior. In Emily Brontë's classic novel *Wuthering Heights*, we read that "He was donned in his Sunday garments, with his most sanctimonious and sourest face."

VOCIFERATE is a verb that means to speak, complain, or argue in a loud or shouting voice. In Stephen Crane's *The Red Badge of Courage*, we read that "Loud and vociferous congratulations were showered upon the maiden."

Write two good sentences for each word.

CAESAR'S ANALOGIES: Find the most similar pairs.

WINNER : MAGNANIMOUS ::
    a. tortuous : road
    b. relic : sacrosanct
    c. conversation : retort
    d. scholar : perspicacious

SANCTIMONIOUS : HUMILITY ::
    a. magnanimous : generous
    b. vocal : vociferous
    c. vociferous : taciturnity
    d. torturous : painful

CAESAR'S ANTONYMS: Find the best opposite.

PERSPICACITY
    a. anachronism
    b. magnanimity
    c. vociferous
    d. obtuseness

TORTUOUS
    a. animal
    b. simple
    c. automatic
    d. torturous

CAESAR'S CONTEXT: Find the best word to complete the sentence.

By exculpating the leader, Caesar showed his _____.
    a. retort
    b. animadversion
    c. invocation
    d. magnanimity

The _____ crowd gathered in the street and raised a clamor.
    a. vociferous
    b. magnanimous
    c. perspicacious
    d. sanctimonious

The fleeing band had to _____ across half of Europe.
    a. vociferate
    b. sanction
    c. peregrinate
    d. percolate

CAESAR'S MATHEMATICS

An eccentric centurion gave a tortuous claim of his innocence to XXVI of his fellow soldiers. VIII of these felt he was being sanctimonious and walked away indignantly. VII of the remaining friends vociferated with him to admit his guilt in the matter, and when he refused, they walked away, acutely vexed. IV of the remaining friends felt that the situation had become irrevocable and fell down prostrate. The remaining friends were perspicacious and magnanimous and forgave the centurion. How many forgave him?

CAESAR'S ESSAY

We love essays because they allow us to write beautifully clear explanations of meaningful things that we care about. Essays have a clear central focus that unites every section into a single, unified whole. You introduce the idea in the introduction, develop that idea in the body, and show what all of the evidence means in the conclusion. It is a fine art of the mind to write a good essay.

We also admire essays because they do not express our opinions. They are not personal guesses or preferences. They are attempts to get it right, to present the actual facts of a matter—the truth—regardless of our preferences. Sometimes the truth is not what we wish, but it is the truth. That is the intellectual integrity of the essay, and that is one of the reasons that good style in a formal academic essay omits first person and self-reference. The essay is about the knowledge, not about ourselves. Find a topic concerning ancient Rome, and write a short essay, practicing the avoidance of all first person and all self-reference and making use of some of our best vocabulary in the process. You may use words from Lessons I through XVII.

CAESAR'S WORD SEARCH

In the puzzle, find the Latin-based English words that you see below. They might be vertical, horizontal, or diagonal. Always notice the stems that are in the words.

S	F	Y	T	I	C	I	L	E	F	A	C	R	E	V
U	A	P	H	G	I	F	V	E	R	D	U	R	E	R
O	F	E	T	A	P	L	U	C	X	E	S	R	S	O
U	L	R	U	U	R	B	A	N	E	Y	U	U	C	M
R	E	S	H	I	U	O	P	R	D	U	O	E	B	A
G	O	P	J	R	F	Y	R	B	X	M	I	T	R	L
N	R	I	X	R	A	U	E	V	I	Y	N	A	H	E
O	T	C	C	E	M	V	T	N	S	N	O	R	Y	V
C	H	A	E	V	B	N	A	X	U	O	M	E	T	O
N	O	C	T	O	I	N	R	F	O	M	I	F	Y	L
I	D	I	Y	C	G	G	T	R	U	I	T	I	R	E
M	O	T	K	A	U	U	S	W	T	R	C	C	W	N
A	X	Y	M	B	O	P	O	A	R	C	N	O	E	C
E	W	P	L	L	U	M	R	Y	O	A	A	V	T	E
X	A	R	P	E	S	I	P	G	T	J	S	D	E	K

perspicacity	incongruous	prostrate	acrimony
magnanimous	malevolence	exculpate	verdure
tortuous	ambiguous	impugn	orthodox
sanctimonious	felicity	urbane	irrevocable
vociferate			

1. Which of these words is the most interesting?
2. Which of these words will you use most often?
3. Which two words are related to each other in some way?
4. Which word sounds most scholarly or academic?
5. Which word has the most precise meaning?

CAESAR'S CLASSIC WORDS CHALLENGE

If we want to get a feel for how words are used, we must see how great writers use words. In each case below, one of the choices was the word used by the author. For you, this is a word game. Your challenge is to guess which word the author used. This is not a test; it is a game because more than one word choice may work perfectly well. See if you can use your sensitivity and intuition to guess which word the author used. You may need a dictionary.

1. From Nathaniel Hawthorne's *The Scarlet Letter*

    It excited neither surprise nor _____.
    a. retort
    b. perspicacity
    c. invocation
    d. animadversion

2. From Thomas Hardy's *The Return of the Native*

    [He] indulged in this imaginary _____ for some considerable interval.
    a. invocation
    b. peregrination
    c. perspicacity
    d. retort

3. From H.G. Wells's *The Invisible Man*

    He became aware of a tumultuous _____.
    a. animadversion
    b. peregrination
    c. invocation
    d. vociferation

CAESAR'S GRAMMAR · CLAUSES

The first three sentences below are worked out for you. See if you can solve the next three, identifying the parts of speech, parts of sentence, phrases, and clauses for each sentence.

1. **Vociferating** his views was a relief; Caesar congratulated him.
   n.   adj.   n.   v.   adj. n.   n.   v.   pron.
   ----------------subj.---------------- LVP   S.C.   subj.   AVP   D.O.
   -----------gerund phrase-----------
   ----------------------------independent clause---------------------- --------------independent clause------------
   Note: This is a compound declarative sentence containing two independent clauses: I;I.

2. Following the **tortuous** path, Gurth gave Ogg a stern look.
   adj.   adj.   adj.   n.   n.   v.   n.   adj. adj. n.
                                       subj. AVP I.O.   D.O.
   ------------------participial phrase------------------
   ---independent clause--
   Note: This is a simple declarative sentence.

3. The seer was **sanctimonious** when Caesar ignored him.
   adj. n.   v.   adj.   conj.   n.   v.   pron.
   subj. LVP   S.C.   subj.   AVP   D.O.
                                no phrases
   -----------------------independent clause----------------- ----------------dependent clause------------------
   Note: This is an ID complex sentence. We do not use a comma to separate the clauses in an ID structure.

4. Caesar enjoyed **articulating** ideas as he wrote his account.
   n   v   adj   n   conj pron v   adj   n
   subj   AVP   DO
   independent   no phrase   dependent

5. Speaking **magnanimously**, Caesar smiled as he held the sword.
   noun   adj   noun   v   conj pron v   adj   noun
                            subj   AVP
   gerund
   independent   independent

6. As his indifference increased, his **perspicacity** started losing clarity.
   con adj   noun   v   adj   n   v   adv   n
                      prepositional subj   AVP   do
   independent   independent

Here is a four-level analysis of a sentence using the noun *perspicacity*, which means brilliant insight.

	They finally understood the **perspicacity** of the strategy.

Parts of Speech:	pron.	adv.	v.	adj.	n.	prep.	adj.	n.

Parts of Sentence:	subj.		AVP		D.O.			

Phrases:						---prep. phrase---		

Clauses:	one independent clause; a simple declarative sentence

This sentence is called simple in structure because it contains only one clause, which is built around the subject/predicate set *they/understood*. In this sentence, the noun *perspicacity* is modified by the adjective *the*, and it serves as the direct object, receiving the action of the action verb *understood*.

One of the secrets of advanced vocabulary is knowing how to alter words in order to use them as different parts of speech. Pick one example from each column below, and write a good sentence using it.

noun	adjective	verb	adverb
perspicacity	perspicacious	-	perspicaciously
retort	-	retort	-
-	sanctimonious	-	sanctimoniously
vociferation	vociferous	vociferate	vociferously
animadversion	-	animadvert	-
peregrination	-	peregrinate	-
-	tortuous	-	tortuously
torture	torturous	torture	torturously

AFTER THE FALL
Michael Clay Thompson

In the first century after the fall,
wind-cold carved cracks in the rocks,
and summer suns seared the columns,
baking polished surfaces dull and gray.
Fine dust fell from bas-reliefs.

In the second century after the fall,
the acrimonious rains of a hundred seasons soaked the roof,
trickling into cracks and wearing cuts smooth.
Drops dripped into the damp interior.
Winds whistled in the crumbling eaves.

In the third century after the fall,
decades of clouds and fogs and mists
seeped into the seams, breaking off chunks
and loosening joints.

In the fourth century after the fall,
a sanctimonious fool broke off pieces
for his grimy hovel and field walls.
He laughed malevolently at the stupid Romans.

In the fifth century after the fall,
some mortified somebody vociferated about
keeping the ruins up. Everyone turned away.
Shepherds found sheep-shelter from storms.

In the next ten centuries after the fall,
a thousand years of profane winds and rains and gales
and thunders and lightnings and snows and tumult and verdure
and muds and fires and wars and vexing fools and insults
and altercations battered the building. It still stands.
That is the germane point.

Photo by Dr. Thomas Milton Kemnitz

THE ROMAN WORLD

We study English vocabulary, passing quickly over reminders that much of our advanced vocabulary is a mouthing of surviving fragments of Latin, the language of the ancient Romans. In this process, it is easy to lose perspective of the truth. Roman history, with its incredible architecture, poetry, law, and military events, can begin to feel like a myth. It was no myth.

Roman civilization was so powerful that 2,000 years later we are still speaking, especially in academic English vocabulary, Roman sounds. The infusion of Roman customs changed Western civilization profoundly and permanently. Roman civilization was urbane, massive, mighty, and extraordinarily successful. The Romans developed highly organized forms of military strategy and tactics that allowed them to subjugate virtually all of the world they knew, only in the end to fall themselves as a result of vexing failures of character: greed, luxury, short-sightedness, acrimony, corruption, nepotism. As Lord Acton, the English historian, said, power corrupts. It is a germane point that these same ignominious failings that disrupted Roman power have brought most civilizations low far faster. The Romans conquered their known world and held it for centuries.

From high in space, we see the story in a glance. All of the great locations of ancient history seem close together, with easily navigable seas and rivers for mariners to sail. We see the Greek peninsula and the Aegean Sea, the great Mediterranean Sea wrapping around Italy, Hispania (a major granary for Rome and the birthplace of five Roman emperors) on the left and Asia Minor on the right. Here is where the city of Rome is, here Athens, here the strait where Constantinople was founded. We see England in the damp northwest and strain to make out Hadrian's Wall. We see Gaul, which Caesar conquered and then had to reconquer. We see fierce Germania to Gaul's east, where three Roman legions were annihilated and where the Anglo-Saxon foundation of English emerged. Far to the north we see Denmark's Jutland peninsula, where the Cimbri lived before migrating south to destroy Roman legions in Aurasio. Here is Sicily, here Crete, here Macedon where Alexander was born hundreds of years before Rome became Rome. We see the cape in northern Africa where Carthage emerged, and we trace with our eyes Hannibal's tortuous path through Hispania, then east over the Alps, then down into Italy to his doleful end.

Rome was no myth, and in our very words we find the crumbled but audible fragments of the words the Romans spoke.

SUBJUGATE

REVIEW FOR CUMULATIVE QUIZ

com	together	**vita**	life	**intra**	within	**vid**	look	**cent**	100
pater	father	**ad**	to	**matri**	mother	**fer**	carry	**pop**	people
loco	place	**sur**	over	**alter**	other	**contra**	against	**stell**	star
amat	love	**luna**	moon	**greg**	group	**clam**	cry out	**tang**	touch
mar	sea	**junct**	join	**luc**	light	**medi**	middle	**tempor**	time
grat	pleasing	**curr**	run	**trans**	across	**migr**	wander	**rupt**	break
clud	close	**se**	apart	**plu**	more	**germ**	vital	**fus**	pour
culp	blame	**pugn**	fight	**urb**	city	**numer**	number	**acr**	sharp
per	through	**anim**	mind	**tort**	twist	**sanct**	holy	**voc**	voice

placate	to appease	commandeer	officially take control
derision	ridicule	intramural	within an institution
vivacious	full of life	centennial	of a 100th anniversary
procure	to acquire	*ad infinitum*	again and again forever
retort	a quick, clever reply	infer	conclude from evidence
vitality	strength, energy	audible	able to be heard
videlicet (viz.)	namely	benevolent	charitable
paternal	of the father	somber	gloomy
matriarch	female head of family	prostrate	lying flat
populous	densely populated	profuse	abundant
localized	restricted to a place	surfeit	an excessive amount
altercation	a noisy argument	contrary	the opposite
stellar	of a star	ostentatious	showy
inexorable	inevitable	indolent	lazy
doleful	mournful	alacrity	eagerness
amatory	romantic	sublunar	under the moon
aggregate	a collected mass	declaim	speak against
entangled	snared, involved	oblique	indirect or slanting
pensive	thoughtful	magnanimous	generous
importune	to pester	peremptory	dictatorial
mariner	a sailor	adjunct	an unessential addition
elucidate	to explain	mediate	to intervene
temporize	to delay	tacit	unspoken
affable	friendly	sanguine	cheerfully confident
torpid	sluggish	mortify	profoundly humiliate
gratuitous	uncalled for	concur	to agree
transcend	to go beyond limits	migratory	moving seasonally
disruption	a disturbing interruption	obsequious	cringing, submissive
ignominy	disgrace	acquiescence	passive compliance
impassive	expressionless, without emotion	impending	about to happen
preclude	prevent	seclude	isolate from people
nonplussed	confused	germane	relevant
infusion	an inpouring	verdure	vegetation
equivocal	ambiguous	orthodox	traditional
profane	irreverent	tumult	disturbance
exculpate	to free from blame	impugn	to dispute the truth
urbane	refined	enumerate	to list
acrimony	bitterness	incongruous	incompatible
malevolence	ill will	ambiguous	uncertain
felicity	great happiness	irrevocable	unalterable
perspicacity	keen insight	tortuous	twisted
sanctimonious	self-righteous	vociferate	argue loudly

Photo by Dr. Thomas Milton Kemnitz

Roman roof tiles from Pompeii

LESSON XVIII · CLASSIC WORDS

English	*Spanish*
adjacent: adjoining	*adyacente*
transient: existing briefly	*transeúnte*
latent: present but inactive	*latente*
livid: bruised or pale	*lívido*
censure: strong criticism	*censura*

ADJACENT (ad-JAY-sent)

The English adjective *adjacent* comes from the Latin *adjecere*, to lie near. *Adjacent* means nearby or adjoining. Something can be adjacent without actually being in contact, unlike being contiguous, which requires contact. In *Silent Spring*, Rachel Carson wrote that "regardless of what citrus growers do, they are more or less at the mercy of the owners of adjacent acreages, for severe damage has been done by insecticidal drift." In *The Yearling*, Marjorie Kennan Rawlings wrote that the "hens laid their eggs all over the adjacent woods, in brierberry tangles, under piles of brush, and the snakes ate as many as the hens hatched." In Jack London's *White Fang*, "he led the pack many a wild chase through the adjacent woods." In H.G. Wells's *The War of the Worlds*, "evolution had taken the same direction in the two adjacent planets." And in William Shakespeare's *Romeo and Juliet*, there are "the demesnes that there adjacent lie."

TRANSIENT (TRAN-see-ent)

Our English adjective *transient* comes from the Latin *transire*, to go across. The noun form is *transience*. *Transient* means existing briefly, passing quickly. In *Silent Spring,* Rachel Carson described "the vetch and the clover and the wood lily in all their delicate and transient beauty." James Hilton wrote in *Lost Horizon* that "it seemed to him that all the loveliest things were transient and perishable." In her novel *Silas Marner,* George Eliot wrote that "The transient fears of the company were now forgotten in their strong curiosity." Robert Louis Stevenson described "the mistlike transience of this seemingly so solid body" in *Dr. Jekyll and Mr. Hyde.* And in *Pride and Prejudice,* Jane Austen wrote that "his attentions to Jane had been merely of a common and transient liking, which ceased when he saw her no more." Which of these sentences do you like the best?

LATENT (LAY-tent)

In ancient Rome, the Latin verb *latere* meant to lie hidden. The English adjective *latent* means present but inactive and therefore potentially hidden. The noun form is *latency.* In *Silent Spring,* Rachel Carson wrote that "a long period of latency is common to most malignancies." In *Native Son,* Richard Wright wrote that "he felt a certain sense of power, a power born of a latent capacity to live." Edith Wharton, in *Ethan Frome*, wrote that "his unhappiness roused his latent fears." In *Billy Budd,* Herman Melville wrote that "he was not without some latent misgiving." There is "a quiet depth of malice, hitherto latent" in Nathaniel Hawthorne's *The Scarlet Letter.* One of the best examples of *latent* comes from John F. Kennedy in *Profiles in Courage*; Kennedy wrote that Daniel Webster had the "ability to make alive and supreme the latent sense of oneness, of Union, that all Americans felt but which few could express." What did Kennedy mean by a "latent sense of oneness"?

LIVID (LIV-id)

Our English adjective *livid* traces back to the Latin verb *livere*, to be blue. It can mean black and blue, bruised-looking, reddish, or even ashen or pallid; it all depends on the context. In H.G. Wells's *The War of the Worlds*, there is "a wide expanse of livid color cut with purple shadows, and very painful to the eye." In *Dracula*, Bram Stoker described "a livid white face bending over me out of the mist." In *The Prince and the Pauper,* Mark Twain described London Bridge, with "the livid and decaying heads of renowned men impaled upon iron spikes atop of its gateways." One of the most famous *livid* sentences comes from Robert Louis Stevenson, who in *Treasure Island* described a pirate "and the sabre cut across one cheek, a dirty, livid white." In Charlotte Brontë's *Jane Eyre,* there are "clouds low and livid, rolling over a swollen sea." Walt Whitman, whose *Leaves of Grass* revolutionized poetry, wrote that "My hurts turn livid upon me as I lean on a cane and observe."

CENSURE (SEN-shure)

The English word *censure*, which comes from the Latin *censura*, can be a noun or a verb, and it refers to strong criticism, such as an official reprimand. John F. Kennedy discussed, in *Profiles in Courage*, a courageous man's observation: "I have no doubt of incurring much censure and obloquy for this measure." In George Orwell's *Animal Farm*, "he had been censured for showing cowardice in the battle." In Jane Austen's *Pride and Prejudice,* a character says, "I would not wish to be hasty in censuring any one; but I always speak what I think." Benjamin Franklin wrote in his *Autobiography* that someone was "taken up, censured, and imprisoned for a month by the Speaker's warrant." In Jonathan Swift's *Gulliver's Travels,* Gulliver is afraid of "being censured as tedious and trifling." In *Hamlet,* Shakespeare has a fool, Polonius, instruct his son to "Take each man's censure, but reserve thy judgment." If everyone did what Polonius asks, what would happen?

REVIEW WORDS FROM *CAESAR'S ENGLISH I*

apprehension: fear
superfluous: extra
tangible: touchable
lurid: sensational
pervade: spread throughout

CAESAR'S MATHEMATICS

XXXVII new laws provided tangible benefits to the citizens of Rome. Another XVI laws provided benefits for tribal areas in Gaul. The effects of these laws pervaded the Empire. Unfortunately, the benefits were transient. Lurid rumors caused VI laws to be repealed. Superfluous monies evaporated, causing V laws to be canceled for lack of funds. A report of corruption caused IV laws to receive official censure, and they also were terminated. How many beneficial laws remained?

ADJACENT

CAESAR'S WORD SEARCH

In the puzzle, find the Latin-based English words that you see below. They might be vertical, horizontal, or diagonal. Always notice the stems that are in the words.

L	W	Q	E	T	A	R	E	F	I	C	O	V	E	R
I	N	C	O	N	G	R	U	O	U	S	A	P	T	P
V	E	E	C	N	E	L	O	V	E	L	A	M	Y	E
I	R	T	Y	S	D	F	G	X	J	K	L	P	T	R
D	W	T	A	N	G	I	B	L	E	H	H	O	N	V
R	A	P	E	G	A	M	C	E	N	S	U	R	E	A
T	N	E	C	A	J	D	A	K	E	D	J	I	T	D
D	T	R	A	N	S	I	E	N	T	F	D	W	A	E
I	R	S	U	O	U	T	R	O	T	O	T	S	L	X
R	Y	D	S	M	A	G	N	A	N	I	M	O	U	S
U	Y	P	E	R	S	P	I	C	A	C	I	T	Y	A
L	T	A	O	W	Y	L	G	O	Z	R	A	L	M	D
S	A	N	C	T	I	M	O	N	I	O	U	S	I	R
L	U	L	N	O	I	S	N	E	H	E	R	P	P	A
T	S	U	O	U	L	F	R	E	P	U	S	V	O	T

adjacent

transient

latent

livid

censure

apprehension

superfluous

tangible

lurid

perspicacity

magnanimous

tortuous

sanctimonious

vociferate

incongruous

malevolence

pervade

1. Which of these words has the most beautiful sound?
2. Which of these words will you see in novels?
3. Which word is most unusual?
4. Which word is the most scholarly or academic?
5. Which word has the most exact meaning?

CAESAR'S CLASSIC WORDS CHALLENGE

If we want to get a feel for how words are used, we must see how great writers use words. In each case below, one of the choices was the word used by the author. For you, this is a word game. Your challenge is to guess which word the author used. This is not a test; it is a game because more than one word choice may work perfectly well. See if you can use your sensitivity and intuition to guess which word the author used. You may need a dictionary.

1. From Stephen Crane's *The Red Badge of Courage*

    The youth turned, with sudden, _____ rage, toward the battlefield.
    a. adjacent
    b. transient
    c. latent
    d. livid

2. From Eudora Welty's *One Writer's Beginnings*

    Photography taught me...to be able to capture _____.
    a. censure
    b. latency
    c. adjacence
    d. transience

3. From George Eliot's *Silas Marner*

    Ravelow was not a place where moral _____ was severe.
    a. censure
    b. latency
    c. adjacence
    d. transience

CAESAR'S GRAMMAR · CLAUSES

The first three sentences below are worked out for you. See if you can solve the next three, identifying the parts of speech, parts of sentence, phrases, and clauses for each sentence.

1. Shedding **superfluous** supplies, the legion hurried toward the valley.
   adj.   adj.   n.   adj.   n.   v.   prep.   adj.   n.
                                                 subj. AVP
   ------------participial phrase------------   -----prepositional phrase-----
   ---------------------------------------independent clause---------------------------------------
   Note: This is one independent clause, a simple sentence. The phrases are part of the clause, as always.

2. The coins were a **tangible** reward; distributing them was difficult.
   adj. n.   v. adj. adj.   n.   n.   pron.   v.   adj.
        subj. LVP   S.C.   ------------subj.------------ LVP S.C.
                                         ---------gerund phrase--------
   -----------------independent clause----------------   -----------------independent clause-----------------
   Note: This is an I;I compound declarative sentence.

3. As the **lurid** lie **pervaded** Rome, Caesar tried silencing the crowd.
   conj. adj. adj. n.   v.   n.   n.   v.   n.   adj.   n.
              subj.   AVP   D.O.   subj. AVP   ------------------D.O.-------------
                                                        -----------gerund phrase---------
   ------------------------dependent clause-------------------   ----------------independent clause-------------------
   Note: This is a D,I complex declarative sentence. We use a comma to separate the clauses in a D,I structure.

4. Feeling **apprehension**, Decius was alarmed, and he gave us signs.

5. Caesar hated receiving **censure**; he angrily defied the Senate.

6. As the **latent** resentment surfaced, they began arming themselves.

Here is a four-level analysis of a sentence using the adjective *transient*, which refers to something that exists only for a brief time.

	It	was	only	**transient**,	but	Caesar	saw	it.
Parts of Speech:	pron.	v.	adv.	adj.	conj.	n.	v.	pron.
Parts of Sentence:	subj.	LVP		S.C.		subj.	AVP	D.O.

Phrases: no prepositional, appositive, or verbal phrases

Clauses: --------independent clause-------- ----indep. clause----
an I,ccI compound declarative sentence

Here the adjective *transient* modifies the pronoun *it*, which is a third person singular subject pronoun. Notice that it is difficult for an adjective to modify a pronoun without being a subject complement; we cannot say *the transient it*, but we can say *it is transient*.

One of the secrets of advanced vocabulary is knowing how to alter words in order to use them as different parts of speech. Pick one example from each column below, and write a good sentence using it.

noun	adjective	verb	adverb
adjacence	adjacent	-	-
transience	transient	-	transiently
latency	latent	-	latently
lividness	livid	-	lividly
censure	censured	censure	-
superfluity	superfluous	-	superfluously

MARCUS AURELIUS
Michael Clay Thompson

Cold night. Firelight tremulous.
Marcus, impassive, huddled with officers
and showed bold plans in sublunar frost.
The vociferous Germans had massed upslope,
up there, in "them trees," Gaius sputtered.
Marcus, magnanimous, did not laugh.

Cold night. Marcus ordered a legion behind a hill
with command of silence. Secluded. No fires.
Tomorrow they'd unroll the loathed Germans' flank.
Hit 'em on the end. A forest attack.

Cold night. Their breaths took flight in the chill,
and officers, somber, strode into the still night.
They needed benevolent quiet after today's battle.
Dismissed. Departing footsteps, bright rattle of armor.

Cold night. His mind serene,
Marcus sat to write meditations.
In Greek. He liked Greek. It was pensive.
Soft sounds, *philos* and *sophos*.
Latin for war, Greek for philosophy.
"The best revenge," he consoled,
"is not to be like your enemy."

Cold night. Across the bold clatter of camp,
lurid fires glowed, and prostrate soldiers,
audible, told old soldier slogans.
Someone affable laughed over there.
Tomorrow, Marcus thought,
we won't be laughing.

The happiness of your life
depends upon
the quality of
your thoughts.

- Marcus Aurelius

THE COLOSSUS OF RHODES

Rhodes is a Greek island in the eastern Aegean Sea, northeast of Crete and southeast of Athens. It is almost adjacent to Asia Minor, being separated by a narrow passage. Pointing obliquely to the northeast, Rhodes is about fifty miles long and twenty-five miles wide. The island was inhabited by Neolithic tribes, by the Carians, by the Phoenecians, by the Minoans, by the Mycenaean Greeks, by the Persians, and by the inexorable Alexander the Great, to name a few. The peremptory Romans eventually took Rhodes under their control; in 164 they forced Rhodes to acquiesce and become what was called a "permanent ally." After Julius Caesar's assassination, the malevolent Cassius destroyed Rhodes and removed thousands of works of art from the prostrate city.

The Colossus of Rhodes—one of the Seven Wonders of the Ancient World—was a ninety-eight-foot-high bronze statue built from 292 to 280 B.C. in the city of Rhodes at the northeast tip of the island. In legend the statue was so enormous that ships sailed between its feet to enter the harbor, but it may in fact have stood on one side of the harbor. The statue was constructed to honor a military victory in which Rhodes defeated Cyprus; the ruler of Cyprus's son had laid siege to Rhodes in 305 B.C. After towering over the harbor for fifty-six years, the colossus was toppled by an earthquake in 226 B.C. The earthquake broke the statue at the knees, and it collapsed over onto the land.

The Colossus of Rhodes served as an inspiration for the Statue of Liberty, and it is alluded to in Emma Lazarus's pensive poem that adorns the pedestal of the Statue of Liberty: "Not like the brazen giant of Greek fame...."

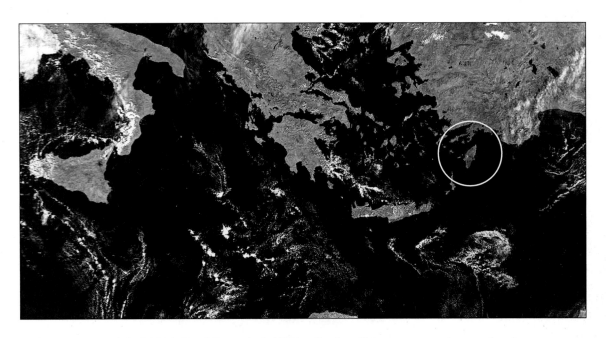

RHODES

CAESAR'S SESQUIPEDALIAN STORY

A lurid incredulity pervaded the somber streets of the capital, and even the most ardent Roman patriots manifested apprehension at the inexorable approach of the barbarians. Transient rumors had swept away sagacious circumspection, and now everyone expected Rome to be overrun by the profane, vulgar, ostentatious Visigoths, a surreal mob more than an army, with odious countenances and grotesque horned helmets—their bearded visages peeking through the faceplates. For weeks, the rumors of impending invasion had not abated, and subtle signs showed that citizens were packing their most treasured belongings and leaving the city before the barbarians arrived. But it was tedious waiting, and some resorted to condescending humor, heaping the barbarians with derision.

There was vexing tangible evidence that the rumors were true. Refugees were stumbling into Rome with vivid, melancholy tales of horror. The orthodox confidence that the malevolent barbarians could never enter Rome had begun to abate—it was prodigiously incongruous with the facts—and the most obsequious citizens were heard practicing their acquiescent welcoming speeches, profusely importuning the implacable barbarians to be magnanimous, and preparing to prostrate themselves affably at the barbarians' feet. Others prepared impassively for martyrdom, pallidly clamoring that they would fight the invaders in every street of the city, that they venerated their homeland. Others showed tacit submission to fate, grew indolent, or became equivocal out of mistrust. No one, really, was sanguine; no one doubted that the tumult was coming.

But at this point, further defensive efforts were superfluous; nothing else could be done. The ignominious barbarians were even now traversing the undulating hills of adjacent regions, awakening latent incredulity, and pensive citizens lost their amiable felicity as they grasped the irrevocable loss of the empire that was Rome. And the future? It was perplexing, an ambiguous abyss.

They made a desert
and called it peace.

- Tacitus

Photo by Dr. Thomas Milton Kemnitz

313

REVIEW FOR CUMULATIVE QUIZ

com	together	**vita**	life	**intra**	within
vid	look	**cent**	one hundred	**pater**	father
ad	to	**matri**	mother	**fer**	carry
pop	people	**loco**	place	**sur**	over
alter	other	**contra**	against	**stell**	star
amat	love	**luna**	moon	**greg**	group
clam	cry out	**tang**	touch	**mar**	sea
junct	join	**luc**	light	**medi**	middle
tempor	time	**grat**	pleasing	**curr**	run
trans	across	**migr**	wander	**rupt**	break
clud	close	**se**	apart	**plu**	more
germ	vital	**fus**	pour	**culp**	blame
pugn	fight	**urb**	city	**numer**	number
acr	sharp	**per**	through	**anim**	mind
tort	twist	**sanct**	holy	**voc**	voice

placate	to appease	**commandeer**	officially take control
derision	ridicule	**intramural**	within an institution
vivacious	full of life	**centennial**	of a 100th anniversary
procure	to acquire	*ad infinitum*	again and again forever
retort	a quick, clever reply	**infer**	conclude from evidence
vitality	strength, energy	**audible**	able to be heard
videlicet (viz.)	namely	**benevolent**	charitable
paternal	of the father	**somber**	gloomy
matriarch	female head of family	**prostrate**	lying flat
populous	densely populated	**profuse**	abundant
localized	restricted to a place	**surfeit**	an excessive amount
altercation	a noisy argument	**contrary**	the opposite
stellar	of a star	**ostentatious**	showy
inexorable	inevitable	**indolent**	lazy
doleful	mournful	**alacrity**	eagerness
amatory	romantic	**sublunar**	under the moon
aggregate	a collected mass	**declaim**	speak against
entangled	snared, involved	**oblique**	indirect or slanting
pensive	thoughtful	**magnanimous**	generous
importune	to pester	**peremptory**	dictatorial
mariner	a sailor	**adjunct**	an unessential addition
elucidate	to explain	**mediate**	to intervene

temporize	to delay	**tacit**	unspoken
affable	friendly	**sanguine**	cheerfully confident
torpid	sluggish	**mortify**	profoundly humiliate
gratuitous	uncalled for	**concur**	to agree
transcend	to go beyond limits	**migratory**	moving seasonally
disruption	a disturbing interruption	**obsequious**	cringing, submissive
ignominy	disgrace	**acquiescence**	passive compliance
impassive	expressionless, without emotion	**impending**	about to happen
preclude	prevent	**seclude**	isolate from people
nonplussed	confused	**germane**	relevant
infusion	an inpouring	**verdure**	vegetation
equivocal	ambiguous	**orthodox**	traditional
profane	irreverent	**tumult**	disturbance
exculpate	to free from blame	**impugn**	to dispute the truth
urbane	refined	**enumerate**	to list
acrimony	bitterness	**incongruous**	incompatible
malevolence	ill will	**ambiguous**	uncertain
felicity	great happiness	**irrevocable**	unalterable
perspicacity	keen insight	**tortuous**	twisted
sanctimonious	self-righteous	**vociferate**	argue loudly
adjacent	adjoining	**transient**	existing briefly
latent	present but inactive	**livid**	bruised or pale
censure	strong criticism		

RETORT

Vesuvius, seen from Pompeii

When they are silent,
they cry out.

- Cicero

LESSON XIX · LATIN STEMS

stem	meaning	modern examples	Spanish
punct	point	punctuate, punctual, punctilious	*puntilloso*
trib	pay	tribute, distribute, contribute	*contribuir*
cap	take	capture, captivate, captious	*capcioso*
pond	weight	ponder, preponderance, ponderous	*ponderoso*
rect	right	correct, rectilinear, rectitude	*rectitud*

PUNCT means point. To *punctuate* is to insert periods, exclamation points, and other symbols into writing; *punctual* means at the appointed time; and *punctilious* means observing points of correct behavior.

TRIB means pay. A *tribute* is the paying of honor; to *distribute* is to allot something, such as pay; and to *contribute* is to pay or give to a cause.

CAP means take. To *capture* someone is to take him or her prisoner, to *captivate* someone is to take control of his or her fascination, and to be *captious* is to be fault-finding, to say and do things designed to catch someone.

POND means weight. To *ponder* is to reflect on weighty matters, the *preponderance* of the evidence is the bulk of it, and a *ponderous* load is a heavy one.

RECT means right. To *correct* is to change from wrong to right, *rectilinear* means made of straight lines, and *rectitude* is moral uprightness.

REVIEW STEMS FROM *CAESAR'S ENGLISH I*

stem	meaning	modern examples
geo*	earth	geothermal, geophysics, geosynchronous
scope*	look	horoscope, electroscope, periscope
anti*	against	anticline, antibody, antitoxin
intro	into	introduce, introspective, introvert
neo*	new	neologism, neoclassic, neonatal

*These stems came to the Romans from the Greek language.

unicant puncture rectilinear anarchy
sition caparison retribution matricide
usion culpable punctuation transform
epugnant urban patrilineal autodidact
d patronize video punctilio rectangle
mony contribute germinal ponderous
fuse decade oppugn paternalism vital
rate asynchrony autocracy capricious
clude punctuate rectify urbanologist
onic hierarchy decapitate gratuitious
ermicide rectitude tributary populace
ilocal biometric matrilineal germane
nslate numeral capitulate automobile
erance hagiarchy repatriated biology
nctilious evidence gynarchy acridine
le ponder correct distribute autoclave
ate attribute urbanity decimate difuse
congratulate octarchy imponderable
ul autotroph tribute culprit migratory
culpability decagram autocrat secede
onarchy capital punctual numerology

NONFICTION WORDS

Here are five important nonfiction words. You might not hear them often in daily conversation, but you will encounter them frequently in your future academic life. Each word is based on one of the stems in the lesson.

stem	word	definition
punct	**punctilious**	attentive to correct details
trib	**retribution**	payback, punishment
cap	**capitulate**	surrender
pond	**imponderable**	difficult to answer
rect	**rectify**	to make right, correct

PUNCTILIOUS is an adjective that means attentive to fine points of conduct or correct behavior. In *Moby Dick*, Herman Melville describes a "very stately punctilious gentleman." Each of these details or fine points is a *punctilio*.

RETRIBUTION is a noun that means revenge, payback. In Bernard Malamud's *The Natural*, we learn that "Bump didn't like warnings of retribution."

CAPITULATE is a verb that means to surrender, to cease to resist. In Mary Shelley's novel *Frankenstein*, we read about a "man who thus capitulated for his safety."

IMPONDERABLE is an adjective or a noun that means difficult to answer or estimate, difficult to ponder. In Herman Melville's *Moby Dick,* we read, "What things real are there, but imponderable thoughts?"

RECTIFY is a verb that means to correct, to make something right. It might mean correcting an error of fact, but it often refers to a situation in which someone has been wronged. In William Shakespeare's 1611 play *The Tempest*, we read, "Some oracle must rectify our knowledge."

Write two good sentences for each word.

RECTIFY

CAESAR'S ANALOGIES: Find the most similar pairs.

BALLOON : PONDEROUS ::
    a. rectify : correct
    b. delay : punctual
    c. speak : diatribe
    d. burden : heavy

PONDER : IDEA ::
    a. tribute : pay
    b. retribution : vengeance
    c. rectify : mistake
    d. punctilious : conduct

CAESAR'S ANTONYMS: Find the best opposite.

CAPTIVATE
    a. bore
    b. rectify
    c. tedium
    d. punctuate

DIATRIBE
    a. preponderance
    b. euphemism
    c. tribute
    d. speech

CAESAR'S CONTEXT: Find the best word to complete the sentence.

The Roman legions were _____ by the countryside of Gaul.
    a. captivated
    b. pondered
    c. rectified
    d. punctuated

The legions transported their _____ equipment up the mountainside.
    a. captious
    b. punctual
    c. punctilious
    d. ponderous

The barbarian leader delivered a violent _____ against the Romans.
    a. preponderance
    b. rectitude
    c. diatribe
    d. capture

CAESAR'S MATHEMATICS

CCLXXIV punctilious Roman patricians denied entrance to XCVI plebeians at an amphitheater. Half of the plebeians acquiesced, but the others demanded that the injustice be rectified. Of those who demanded rectification, XXXII eventually capitulated, but the acrimonious remainder sought retribution. How many sought retribution?

CAESAR'S ESSAY

One of the beauties of the essay is that it is a format for learning and writing about one of your favorite topics. The topic might not be your favorite before you begin, but as you read and research and accumulate knowledge, you find yourself thinking that the topic is profoundly interesting. Pick an area of Roman history that you think might be interesting. It could be Roman art or poetry, Roman social life or architecture, Roman politics or law, Roman philosophy or military history—anything. Read patiently and with enjoyment until you find something that would be fun to write about, and then write a careful, academic essay about your topic. Remember to use no slang, no contractions, and no first person or self-reference. Be sure to have three sections: an introduction, a body of several paragraphs, and a conclusion. Five paragraphs will be enough, though real essays often have far more than five.

CAPITULATE

CAESAR'S WORD SEARCH

In the puzzle, find the Latin-based English words that you see below. They might be vertical, horizontal, or diagonal. Always notice the stems that are in the words.

S	U	O	I	L	I	T	C	N	U	P	S	F	H	N
E	R	N	Y	U	D	I	R	U	L	I	O	P	N	O
T	R	W	O	S	U	O	I	T	P	A	C	E	T	I
N	K	Q	T	I	U	S	R	H	Y	U	B	L	N	T
E	R	S	C	Y	S	P	O	N	D	E	R	B	E	U
C	J	E	E	U	L	N	E	J	C	V	P	A	I	B
A	L	T	C	D	P	O	E	R	O	T	O	R	S	I
J	E	A	K	T	A	U	U	H	F	P	T	E	N	R
D	T	L	U	E	I	V	X	P	E	L	I	D	A	T
A	R	U	B	T	R	T	R	P	S	R	U	N	R	E
W	I	T	B	I	C	R	U	E	N	A	P	O	T	R
A	B	I	V	E	G	N	I	D	P	A	V	P	U	X
M	U	P	A	R	B	N	U	M	E	P	T	M	A	S
I	T	A	E	F	N	A	P	J	A	C	I	Z	R	
R	E	C	T	I	F	Y	V	T	B	G	I	E	M	S

punctilious	punctual	rectitude	lurid
retribution	tribute	apprehension	pervade
capitulate	captious	superfluous	adjacent
imponderable	ponder	tangible	transient
rectify			

1. Which of these words is the most interesting?
2. Which of these words will you use most often?
3. Which two words are related to each other in some way?
4. Which word sounds most scholarly or academic?
5. Which word has the most precise meaning?

CAESAR'S CLASSIC WORDS CHALLENGE

If we want to get a feel for how words are used, we must see how great writers use words. In each case below, one of the choices was the word used by the author. For you, this is a word game. Your challenge is to guess which word the author used. This is not a test; it is a game because more than one word choice may work perfectly well. See if you can use your sensitivity and intuition to guess which word the author used. You may need a dictionary.

1. From Joseph Heller's *Catch-22*

   He brooded in _____ speculation over the cryptic message.
   a. punctual
   b. ponderous
   c. captious
   d. punctilious

2. From Jane Austen's *Emma*

   I...was too cheerful in my views to be _____.
   a. ponderous
   b. punctual
   c. punctilious
   d. captious

3. From Thomas Hardy's *The Return of the Native*

   It was an error which could never be _____.
   a. captivated
   b. rectified
   c. pondered
   d. punctuated

CAESAR'S GRAMMAR · CLAUSES

The first three sentences below are worked out for you. See if you can solve the next three, identifying the parts of speech, parts of sentence, phrases, and clauses for each sentence.

1. **Capitulating** ignominiously humiliated him; it was mortifying.
   - n. — adv. — v. — pron. — pron. — v. — adj.
   - ------------------------subj.---------------------- AVP — D.O. — subj. — LVP — S.C.
   - ------------------gerund phrase----------------
   - --------------------------------independent clause---------------------------- --------independent clause------

   Note: Notice that an adverb can modify a gerund, even though a gerund is a noun.

2. Because he was **punctilious,** he enjoyed following orders.
   - conj. — pron. — v. — adj. — pron. — v. — n. — n.
   - subj. — LVP — S.C. — subj. — AVP — -------------D.O.------------
   - --------gerund phrase-------
   - ----------------------dependent clause----------------- ---------------------independent clause--------------------

   Note: This is a D,I complex declarative sentence.

3. **Rectifying** the injustice, Caesar gave Casca an apology.
   - adj. — adj. — n. — n. — v. — n. — adj. — n.
   - subj. — AVP — I.O. — D.O.
   - ---------------participial phrase--------------
   - --independent clause---

   Note: This is a simple declarative sentence. The phrase is part of the clause.

4. The **imponderable** problem was difficult; Galen stopped studying it.

5. **Censuring** the senator ended when Caesar gained power.

6. **Impugning** his integrity, Caesar gave Brutus a fierce glance.

Here is a four-level analysis of a sentence using the adjective *captious*, which refers to fault-finding.

	The	**captious**	remark	showed	his	suspicious	attitude.
Parts of Speech:	adj.	adj.	n.	v.	adj.	adj.	n.

Parts of Sentence:			subj.	AVP			D.O.

Phrases: no prepositional, appositive, or verbal phrases

Clauses: one independent clause; a simple declarative sentence

In this sentence, the adjective *captious* modifies the noun *remark*. The sentence contains an action verb *showed*, which transfers the action to the direct object, the noun *attitude*.

One of the secrets of advanced vocabulary is knowing how to alter words in order to use them as different parts of speech. Pick one example from each column below, and write a good sentence using it.

noun	adjective	verb	adverb
-	punctilious	-	punctiliously
-	captious	-	captiously
-	ponderous	ponder	ponderously
censure	censured	censure	-
rectification	rectified	rectify	-
preponderance	preponderant	preponderate	preponderantly
introspection	introspective	introspect	introspectively

EMPRESS THEODORA

Michael Clay Thompson

What? Justinian slink from his palace?
Acquiesce to rebel malice and vamoose, disgraced,
in tremulous cowardice? Not if she had anything
to say about it. What tortuous logic was this?
Oh, no, there would be no obsequious capitulation.
Better to croak in the purple robe
than scram in foggy ignominy.

Retribution? First, save Justinian's power;
then force those sanctimonious blockheads to cower
and rectify their derisions or be martyred.
Before she left this tower, she thought,
these demonstrators would barter
and prostrate themselves before Justinian
and importune him for mercy.
They really think they can commandeer
the reigns of his empire? Really? Too absurd.
Like Phoebus and Phaeton.

Imperious Theodora stormed the halls, on the double,
declaiming, robes flying, shouting trouble,
peremptory. Inexorable—she'd not be contradicted.
One way or other, she'd stay in Constantinople.

There he was. "Justinian, what's this!
Stand up to these indolent stooges.
Assert your status as patriarch of the Empire.
Drop this affable mask; dictate some dread decree.
Send General Belisarius out; choose him,
and he will make those chumps an offer
they can't refuse."

HISPANIA (SPAIN)

In 1000 B.C., Phoenician mariners (from what we call Lebanon) founded the city of Cadiz at the southern tip of the Iberian peninsula, and the city has been inhabited ever since. In 236 B.C., the Carthaginian (Punic) general Hamilcar Barca, the father of Hannibal, invaded Iberia and claimed it as a Carthaginian province. Hannibal became Supreme Commander of Iberia in 221 B.C. and besieged the east coast city of Saguntum, a quasi-independent ally of Rome, inviting Roman retribution and beginning the Second Punic War. Carthaginian control of Iberia would last only two decades.

In 218 B.C. Roman legions marched into the Iberian peninsula, attacked the Carthaginians, commandeered the resources, and began to use what they called *Hispania* as a base for military training. It would take 200 years, until 19 B.C., for Rome, under Augustus, to gain control of the vexing Celtic-Iberians, who refused to capitulate. For the next 500 years, Spain was inexorably pervaded with Roman culture, language, laws, roads, and poetry, with Rome and Hispania exerting profound mutual influences. The Romans divided Hispania into two administrative regions, with a tortuous line running from Carthago Nova (now Cartagena) in the south to the Cantabrian Sea (now the Bay of Biscay) in the north. They called the region most distant from Rome *Hispania Ulterior* and the region closest to Rome *Hispania Citerior*. Later Romans, including Agrippa and Augustus, subdivided the peninsula still further.

One of the results of this extended entanglement was what we know as the Spanish language, a modern offshoot of Latin. This is why Spanish and English, neither of which existed during the peak of Roman civilization, have so many cognates in common. English began as a Germanic language, but the centuries have brought such an infusion of Latin content into academic English that it sometimes seems to be almost as Latinate as Spanish. The two languages are united by thousands of identical or near-identical cognates.

As Myriam Borges Thompson has written in *Caesar's English I*, Hispania was the birthplace of important Roman emperors, including Trajan, Theodosius I, Marcus Aurelius, and Hadrian, as well as important Roman figures such as the rhetorician Quintilian, the perspicacious Seneca, and the poet Martial.

In 409 Germanic tribes, including the Visigoths, entered Hispania, issuing in a period of struggle, followed by the invasion of the Muslims, called Moors, from northern Africa. The Muslims called Hispania *Al-Andalus*, giving rise to the name *Andalusia*. They would control Spain until 1492.

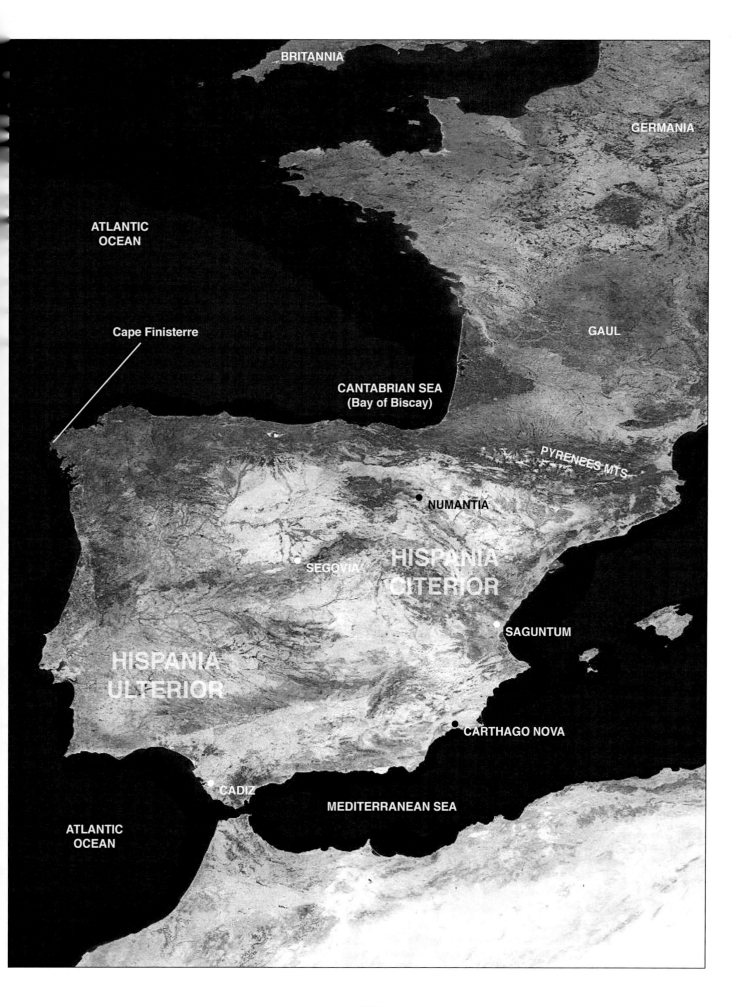

BRITANNIA

GERMANIA

ATLANTIC
OCEAN

GAUL

Cape Finisterre

CANTABRIAN SEA
(Bay of Biscay)

PYRENEES MTS

● NUMANTIA

HISPANIA
CITERIOR

○ SEGOVIA

○ SAGUNTUM

HISPANIA
ULTERIOR

● CARTHAGO NOVA

○ CADIZ

ATLANTIC
OCEAN

MEDITERRANEAN SEA

REVIEW FOR CUMULATIVE QUIZ

com	together	**vita**	life	**intra**	within
vid	look	**cent**	one hundred	**pater**	father
ad	to	**matri**	mother	**fer**	carry
pop	people	**loco**	place	**sur**	over
alter	other	**contra**	against	**stell**	star
amat	love	**luna**	moon	**greg**	group
clam	cry out	**tang**	touch	**mar**	sea
junct	join	**luc**	light	**medi**	middle
tempor	time	**grat**	pleasing	**curr**	run
trans	across	**migr**	wander	**rupt**	break
clud	close	**se**	apart	**plu**	more
germ	vital	**fus**	pour	**culp**	blame
pugn	fight	**urb**	city	**numer**	number
acr	sharp	**per**	through	**anim**	mind
tort	twist	**sanct**	holy	**voc**	voice
punct	point	**trib**	pay	**cap**	take
pond	weight	**rect**	right		

placate	to appease	**commandeer**	officially take control
derision	ridicule	**intramural**	within an institution
vivacious	full of life	**centennial**	of a 100th anniversary
procure	to acquire	*ad infinitum*	again and again forever
retort	a quick, clever reply	**infer**	conclude from evidence
vitality	strength, energy	**audible**	able to be heard
videlicet (viz.)	namely	**benevolent**	charitable
paternal	of the father	**somber**	gloomy
matriarch	female head of family	**prostrate**	lying flat
populous	densely populated	**profuse**	abundant
localized	restricted to a place	**surfeit**	an excessive amount
altercation	a noisy argument	**contrary**	the opposite
stellar	of a star	**ostentatious**	showy
inexorable	inevitable	**indolent**	lazy
doleful	mournful	**alacrity**	eagerness
amatory	romantic	**sublunar**	under the moon
aggregate	a collected mass	**declaim**	speak against
entangled	snared, involved	**oblique**	indirect or slanting
pensive	thoughtful	**magnanimous**	generous
importune	to pester	**peremptory**	dictatorial

mariner	a sailor	**adjunct**	an unessential addition
elucidate	to explain	**mediate**	to intervene
temporize	to delay	**tacit**	unspoken
affable	friendly	**sanguine**	cheerfully confident
torpid	sluggish	**mortify**	profoundly humiliate
gratuitous	uncalled for	**concur**	to agree
transcend	to go beyond limits	**migratory**	moving seasonally
disruption	a disturbing interruption	**obsequious**	cringing, submissive
ignominy	disgrace	**acquiescence**	passive compliance
impassive	expressionless, without emotion	**impending**	about to happen
preclude	prevent	**seclude**	isolate from people
nonplussed	confused	**germane**	relevant
infusion	an inpouring	**verdure**	vegetation
equivocal	ambiguous	**orthodox**	traditional
profane	irreverent	**tumult**	disturbance
exculpate	to free from blame	**impugn**	to dispute the truth
urbane	refined	**enumerate**	to list
acrimony	bitterness	**incongruous**	incompatible
malevolence	ill will	**ambiguous**	uncertain
felicity	great happiness	**irrevocable**	unalterable
perspicacity	keen insight	**tortuous**	twisted
sanctimonious	self-righteous	**vociferate**	argue loudly
adjacent	adjoining	**transient**	existing briefly
latent	present but inactive	**livid**	bruised or pale
censure	strong criticism	**punctilious**	attentive to correct details
retribution	payback, punishment	**capitulate**	surrender
imponderable	difficult to answer	**rectify**	to make right, correct

Photo by Dr. Thomas Milton Kemnitz

LESSON XX · CLASSIC WORDS

English	*Spanish*
epithet: a characterizing term	*epíteto*
abject: miserable	*abyecto*
eccentric: unconventional	*excéntrico*
imperious: overbearing	*imperioso*
solicitude: concern	*solicitud*

EPITHET (EP-ih-thet)

The English noun *epithet* comes from the Latin *epitheton*, which the Romans derived from the Greek *epithetos*. An epithet is a word or phrase that we add to someone's name to characterize him or her; it also can be an abusive word. The most famous epithets are from Homer, as when he referred to gray-eyed Athena in *The Odyssey*. John F. Kennedy wrote in *Profiles in Courage* that "Nine of twenty-two Democratic papers in the state are unbounded in vilifying him with such epithets as traitor, apostate, scoundrel." In *All the King's Men,* Robert Penn Warren wrote that "The juicy epithets had long since lost their fine savor and a strident mechanical quality had crept into the rendering of the scene." Kipling used *epithet* in his 1901 novel *Kim*: "he called it a Moon of Paradise, a Disturber of Integrity, and a few other fantastic epithets which doubled her up with mirth." In *The Red Badge of Courage,* Stephen Crane wrote, "This cold officer upon a monument, who dropped epithets unconcernedly down, would be finer as a dead man, he thought." In Walter Scott's *Ivanhoe*, there is "the same slow pace and listless and indifferent manner which had procured him the epithet of the Black Sluggard," and one character pleads, "Bestow not on me...the epithet of noble."

ABJECT (AB-ject)

The English adjective *abject* comes from the Latin *abjectus*, a form of the verb *abicere,* to cast off. *Abject* means miserable, thrown-down emotionally. Jack London, in *White Fang*, wrote that "White Fang crawled slowly, cringing and groveling in the abjectness of his abasement and submission." In James M. Barrie's *Peter Pan*, we see "Hook in their midst as abject as if he heard the crocodile." Stephen Crane wrote in *The Red Badge of Courage* that "Inwardly he was reduced to an abject pulp by these chance words." In *Frankenstein,* Mary Shelley's monster feels himself reduced to "the lowest degradation, a condition more abject than that of the blind mole or harmless worm." What do you think Joseph Conrad meant in *Lord Jim* by "He commenced by being abjectly lachrymose"? Here is a hint: *lachrymose* means tearful.

ECCENTRIC (eck-SENT-rick)

The English adjective *eccentric* means unconventional, deviating from society's established patterns. The Romans got their Latin word *eccentricus* from the Greek *ekkentros,* out of the center. James Watson, who discovered DNA with Frances Crick, wrote in his autobiographical account *The Double Helix* that "Naomi was a sister of England's most clever and eccentric biologist, J.B.S. Haldane." Neville Shute wrote in *On the Beach* that people behaved "with an eccentricity that verged on madness, born of the times they lived in." In *To Kill a Mockingbird,* Harper Lee wrote that "we came to know Dill as a pocket Merlin whose head teemed with eccentric plans." In *The Time Machine,* H.G. Wells wrote that "My pockets had always puzzled Weena, but...she had concluded that they were an eccentric kind of vase for floral decoration." And in George Orwell's *1984,* he wrote, "It would even have seemed slightly unorthodox, a dangerous eccentricity."

IMPERIOUS (im-PEER-ee-us)

The English adjective *imperious* comes from the Latin *imperiosus* and refers to behavior that is commanding, domineering, overbearing—as though the imperious person is acting like an emperor. Toni Morrison wrote in *Song of Solomon*: "Now she held up her hand, imperiously, and silenced Hagar's whines." In *The Secret Garden,* Burnett wrote, "in the midst of it he had recovered himself and beckoned imperiously to Dickon." In Grahame's *The Wind in the Willows,* we read that "Something up above was calling him imperiously" and that "the wafts from his old home pleaded, whispered, conjured, and finally claimed him imperiously." In *The Call of the Wild,* Jack London described Buck: "Among the terriers he stalked imperiously." And in *Black Beauty,* Anna Sewell wrote, "in an imperious voice she said, 'York, you must put those horses' heads higher, they are not fit to be seen.'"

SOLICITUDE (so-LISS-ih-tood)

The English noun *solicitude* means concern; it suggests the desire to protect. Its adjective form, *solicitous,* comes from the Latin *sollicitus.* In *Profiles in Courage,* John F. Kennedy describes a politician who pretends "extraordinary solicitude for the people." In *The Yearling,* Marjorie Kennan Rawlings wrote that "the convalescence, the solicitude of his mother and his father, was definitely pleasant." A good example comes from Aldous Huxley in *Brave New World*: "'I say,' Helmholtz exclaimed solicitously, 'You do look ill, John!'" In Charles Dickens's *A Tale of Two Cities,* they "tended the wounded man with the gentlest solicitude." Charlotte Brontë wrote in *Jane Eyre* that Jane "felt a conscientious solicitude for Adele's welfare and progress." Can one feel solicitude for a gun? In *The Last of the Mohicans*, James Fenimore Cooper wrote that a character "lifted his rifle, and after regarding it a moment with melancholy solicitude, laid it carefully aside." And in Jane Austen's *Pride and Prejudice*, "Elizabeth looked at her sister with incredulous solicitude." What would incredulous solicitude look like?

REVIEW WORDS FROM *CAESAR'S ENGLISH I*

genial: kind
stolid: unemotional
palpable: touchable
austere: bare
furtive: stealthy

CAESAR'S MATHEMATICS

CDLXXI abject plebeians hurled DCCXXXIX eccentric epithets at CCXLIV imperious patricians. CCCXII of the plebeians subsequently developed feelings of remorseful solicitude and withdrew their remarks. One third of the plebians who remained felt sudden pangs of punctilious courtesy and apologized. Of the remaining two thirds, LXVIII felt that the issues had become imponderable and departed. How many abject but unrepentant plebeians remained?

CAESAR'S WORD SEARCH

In the puzzle, find the Latin-based English words that you see below. They might be vertical, horizontal, or diagonal. Always notice the stems that are in the words.

E	S	C	T	E	R	U	S	N	E	C	A	I	S	D
P	U	D	E	Q	W	G	U	E	L	E	H	M	L	P
C	P	U	V	N	R	E	O	D	B	R	G	P	F	U
E	E	X	N	T	L	E	I	F	I	T	N	O	L	N
D	R	P	O	R	T	C	R	H	G	J	O	N	S	C
U	F	E	I	A	N	C	E	A	N	D	I	D	C	T
T	L	R	S	U	E	E	P	D	A	G	T	E	A	I
I	U	V	N	S	I	N	M	J	T	H	U	R	P	L
C	O	A	E	E	S	T	I	A	U	J	B	A	I	I
I	U	D	H	X	N	R	R	C	N	N	I	B	T	O
L	S	E	E	V	A	I	C	E	I	K	R	L	U	U
O	E	F	R	C	R	C	F	N	L	U	T	E	L	S
S	N	B	P	C	T	E	H	T	I	P	E	I	A	D
M	P	E	P	N	Y	F	I	T	C	E	R	P	T	O
A	X	L	A	B	J	E	C	T	F	B	O	D	E	P

epithet	solicitude	imponderable	tangible
abject	punctilious	rectify	pervade
eccentric	retribution	apprehension	adjacent
imperious	capitulate	superfluous	transient
censure			

1. Which of these words has the most beautiful sound?
2. Which of these words will you see in novels?
3. Which word is most unusual?
4. Which word is the most scholarly or academic?
5. Which word has the most exact meaning?

CAESAR'S CLASSIC WORDS CHALLENGE

If we want to get a feel for how words are used, we must see how great writers use words. In each case below, one of the choices was the word used by the author. For you, this is a word game. Your challenge is to guess which word the author used. This is not a test; it is a game because more than one word choice may work perfectly well. See if you can use your sensitivity and intuition to guess which word the author used. You may need a dictionary.

1. From George Orwell's *1984*

   Thought-criminals made _____ confessions of their crimes.
      a. abject
      b. eccentric
      c. imperious
      d. solicitous

2. From Robert Penn Warren's *All the King's Men*

   She commanded me in a(n) _____ whisper.
      a. abject
      b. eccentric
      c. solicitous
      d. imperious

3. From Thomas Hardy's *The Return of the Native*

   She glanced at him with furtive _____.
      a. abjection
      b. eccentricity
      c. solicitude
      d. epithets

CAESAR'S GRAMMAR · CLAUSES

The first three sentences below are worked out for you. See if you can solve the next three, identifying the parts of speech, parts of sentence, phrases, and clauses for each sentence.

1. Shouting vicious **epithets** was a mistake; everyone disliked him.
        n.   adj.   n.   v. adj. n.   pron.   v.   pron.
   --------------------subj.-------------------- LVP   S.C.   subj.   AVP   D.O.
   --------------gerund phrase-------------
   ----------------------------independent clause----------------------------   --------independent clause-------
   Note: This is an I;I compound declarative sentence.

2. Around the extended and dangerous border, **abject** tribes waited.
    prep. adj.   adj.   conj.   adj.   n.   adj.   n.   v.
                                                            subj.   AVP
   ----------------------------prepositional phrase-------------------------
   --independent clause--
   Note: This is a simple declarative sentence.

3. Feeling **solicitude**, Justinian smiled as the ambassador arrived.
      adj.   n.   n.   v.   conj. adj.   n.   v.
                               subj.   AVP   subj.   AVP
   -----participial phrase--------
   -------------------------independent clause-------------------   ----------------dependent clause----------------
   Note: This is a D,I complex declarative sentence.

4. Cassius enjoyed deceiving Caesar, but this was **malevolent**.
      n   V   n   n   (conj) pron V   adj
    subj avp   DO   subj Lvp sc
             Jirend   Independent
          independent

5. Caesar responded with a **magnanimous** but **imperious** wave.
      n   V   prep adj adj   conj adj   n
    subj avp   prep phrase
        Independent

6. Rejecting **eccentric** inventions, Caesar used a direct strategy.
     adj   adj   n   n   V adj adj   n
     participel   sbj avp   do

Here is a four-level analysis of a sentence using the adjective *abject*, which means miserable, down-thrown.

	Some	barbarians	lived	in	**abject**	submission	to	Rome.
Parts of Speech:	adj.	n.	v.	prep.	adj.	n.	prep.	n.

Parts of Sentence: subj.   AVP

Phrases: ----------prep. phrase---- -prep. phr.-

Clauses: one independent clause; a simple declarative sentence

Here the adjective *abject* modifies the noun *submission*. What is especially interesting about this sentence is the two prepositional phrases after the action verb; notice that there is no direct object. Neither the noun *submission* nor the noun *Rome* can be a direct object because they are objects of prepositions.

One of the secrets of advanced vocabulary is knowing how to alter words in order to use them as different parts of speech. Pick one example from each column below, and write a good sentence using it.

<u>noun</u>	<u>adjective</u>	<u>verb</u>	<u>adverb</u>
abjection	abject	-	abjectly
eccentricity	eccentric	-	eccentrically
solicitude	solicitous	-	solicitously
-	genial	-	genially
palpability	palpable	-	palpably
austerity	austere	-	austerely
furtiveness	furtive	-	furtively

AUGUSTUS, THE BIG A

Michael Clay Thompson

Imperator Gaius Julius Divi
Filius Caesar Octavianus Augustus—
blah blah blah. Just say *Augustus*, the Big *A*,
the Imperious Man. Defeated Brutus
and malevolent Cassius, then Antony.
That's what happens when you underestimate
an impassive, pensive genius. Brought his A game.
He was Caesar's great nephew—so they should've known.
Should have kept a closer eye on 'im. Too late now.
Founded the Empire. Yes, *the*. And the *Pax Romana*.
Those shaggy, nonplussed border clans had to capitulate.
Acquiesce would be too soft a word.
Did I say he killed the Roman Republic?
Yep, by forging the Roman Empire, with his
own august Self as Emperor Augustus.
New rule: you will do it because I say so.
No use impugning A's motives. It happened.
Like Alexander, he changed the Western world.
His august sights were not on tangible wealth,
not on ostentation, but on power,
power that pervaded the Pax.
Power with a capital *p*. Not transient power.
The *Pax Romana* would last two centuries.
Complicated guy. Surfeit of talent.
Could be magnanimous but peremptory,
and he could cast his cold eye on retribution,
so you had to watch it, or he'd make you pay, the Big A.
Somber sometimes. Benevolent sometimes.
Sanctimonious sometimes. All of that.
Augustus: an apt epithet.

I found Rome a city
of bricks and left it
a city of marble.

- Augustus

THE ADRIATIC SEA

The Adriatic Sea is the northernmost branch of the Mediterranean. It is located between the Italian Peninsula and the Balkan Peninsula, which extends southward to Greece. The Adriatic is separated from the Ionian section of the Mediterranean by the Strait of Otranto. The eastern shores of the Adriatic are filled with islands—more than 1,300 of them—along the coast of Croatia and the adjacent region we now call Bosnia and Herzegovina.

In the ancient world, Roman influence pervaded the Adriatic region. The Roman Republic took control of the Adriatic by the second century B.C. In order to prevent Carthaginian mariners from sailing into the Adriatic, the Romans built a strong naval base in Brundisium, which is now called Brindisi. The Romans built a road, the Via Appia, to connect Brundisium to Rome. Roman control of the eastern shores of the Adriatic was not complete until the imperious Augustus's eccentric general Tiberius forced the Illyrians to capitulate in the years 6 to 9 A.D.

Also during Augustus's reign, the Romans developed Ravenna into a major port and naval base; later, in 402 A.D., they moved the capital of the Empire to Ravenna because its surrounding marshes made it more secure from the attacking Germanic tribes. After Rome fell in 476 A.D., the Ostragoths made Ravenna their capital.

Illyria was the western Balkan Peninsula. The Romans began their conquest there in 168 B.C. after what we call the Illyrian Wars. Illyria is an example of a place where there were many great kingdoms of which we have never heard at all, even though they were powerful and important. These were not transient kingdoms; they were enduring. To enumerate: in Illyria there was the kingdom of Bardyllis, of the Dardani, and of Agron of the Ardiaei. The Romans had to defeat the Pannonians and the Daesitiates. Eventually, Rome took control of the western Balkans by defeating and capturing the vexing Gentius, the last king of Illyria. In 165 B.C. the Romans took Gentius ignominiously to Rome in chains.

After the tumultuous subjugation of Illyria into a Roman province, the Romans called the province Illyricum.

ECCENTRIC

CAESAR'S SESQUIPEDALIAN STORY

From the top of the wall, the sentry stood stolid and impassive, steeling himself against the tedium and scanning the darkening verdure for signs of furtive motions. A palpable sense of apprehension that would not abate pervaded the austere encampment, and the abject confessions of yesterday's prisoners fooled no one. The somber soldiers could get little repose on such a night. Caesar's imperious admonitions and his solicitude for the condition of the men made him a genial commander in the men's eyes, but his strategies were always eccentric, unorthodox, and the men often failed to understand the subtle sagacity of his plans until the battle was already won.

Yesterday a vulgar delegation of Gauls from the town had come out, all obsequious and affable, with doleful countenances and lurid, ostentatious trinkets, grotesquely prostrating themselves at Caesar's feet and profusely importuning his benevolence to spare their town—"Venerable Caesar" was their epithet—and he seemed to respond magnanimously. But when they departed, his transient sanguine nature turned pensive, and he issued peremptory orders for the men to ready their weapons. The perspicacious Caesar smelled something incongruous in the amiable remonstrations of the Gauls, a malevolent trap, a sudden attack from the towering forest, and his usually placid visage now seemed almost ambiguous, almost contradicted by melancholy. Treachery made Caesar livid with rage, and the Gauls would suffer something more odious—more inexorable—than censure if they ignominiously broke their assurance.

Pallid and manifestly implacable, Caesar gave orders to build the fires and increase the watch, and all along the watchtower, perplexed sentries kept the view, eyes fixed on the adjacent forest, standing in tacit incredulity that the Gauls would dare to attack the Roman camp. The abyss of darkness grew more profound, almost tangible, and something was audible behind the tree line. A growing tumult was profaning the serenity of the night; a prodigious clamor arose, and then they came, in surreal mobs pouring down the slope, the flaming vivid arrows hurtling obliquely down upon the camp, the cries of the sentries vexing the entire camp into action.

Photo by Dr. Thomas Milton Kemnitz

ARCHITECTURE AND THOUGHT IN HISPANIA
Dr. Myriam Borges Thompson

Roman Hispania is the cultural source of all modern Spanish-speaking cultures, in Latin America and elsewhere. Even though it was remote, Hispania was not an abject backwater. It was the birthplace of imperious Roman emperors and the source of much of Rome's superfluous wealth. Its proud people did not capitulate to Roman domination; it took the Romans 200 years to complete their occupation of this important province. Two examples of the importance of Hispania in Roman history are the Tower of Hercules, an architectural wonder, and Seneca the Younger, a philosophical genius.

The Tower of Hercules

The Farum Brigantium (Tower of Hercules) is a lighthouse built by the Romans at the end of of the first century A.D. The Farum is located in Finisterre in northwestern Spain along the rugged Galician coast. It is on the site where, according to legend, Hercules buried the head of the giant Geryon, and today it is the oldest working lighthouse in the world.

The lighthouse was probably designed by Caio Seio Lupo, an architect from Lusitania in what was once Hispania Ulterior, who left the following inscription at the foot of the tower:

> Marti / (Consecrated to Mars)
> Aug[ustus] Sacr[um] / (Augusto)
> C[aius] Sevius / (Caio Sevio Lupo)
> Architectus / (Architect)
> Lusitanus ex Vo[to] / (Lusitanean in fulfilment of a vow)

The inner core of what remains of the Roman tower is about 125 feet tall and is beneath four walls built in the eighteenth century. On June 27, 2009, for its outstanding nature as a unique testimony to Roman civilization, the Tower of Hercules was declared a UNESCO World Heritage Site, thus becoming the only lighthouse in the World Heritage list that has been in continuous use since Roman times.

Seneca the Younger

"Wherever there is a human being there is an opportunity for kindness."
- Seneca the Younger (4 B.C.-65 A.D.)

Lucio Anneo Seneca was an eccentric philosopher, writer, statesman, and dramatist who is best known for being the perspicacious tutor of the Roman emperor Nero.

Seneca was born in Córdoba in the province of Hispania. His father was a wealthy rhetorician known as Seneca the Elder. Seneca's mother was Helvia, to whom he wrote around 42 A.D. the well-known *Ad Hevia Matrem, De Consolatione* (*To Helvia, On Consolation*). In this work Seneca praised his mother's intelligence, strength of character, and wisdom, but above all, he tried to console Helvia about his exile to Corsica (in 41 A.D. he had been banished from Rome by Emperor Claudius), saying that her character would help her endure his absence. He considered his exile just a change of place that allowed him an opportunity to study and pursue many delights.

The positive outlook of Seneca in the face of his life's trials stood in harmony with the Hellenistic Stoic philosophy he had studied in Rome when he was young. Stoicism taught that people needed to understand and control their passions in order to live with moderation and honesty, accepting the realities of life and death.

To this day, Seneca's name is associated with wisdom and the acceptance of our limitations. It is the view of our mortality not as a tragedy, but as inspiration to have a resilient and fulfilled inner life.

ABJECT

ROMAN MANUFACTURING MIGHT
Dr. Thomas Milton Kemnitz

One of the sources of Rome's power was its success as a manufacturing and trading juggernaut. Prosperity in the Roman Empire was more pervasive than ever before and for more than 1,000 years after. Numerous amenities were available to the inhabitants of Roman towns—tangible amenities that were rare or unknown elsewhere. The basis of Rome's prosperity was concrete. The Romans built what they wanted where they wanted it. The Greeks had to find a hill to build a theater, but the Romans constructed them everywhere using concrete. Towns as small as 20,000 people had their own theater for plays and musicals, as well as an amphitheater or stadium for sporting events or gladiatorial fights.

Concrete enabled the Romans to build roads that lasted—and continue to last 2,000 years later. They could make harbors because they developed concrete that would harden underwater, a technology that would not be recreated until the twentieth century. They could build bridges and causeways that endured and facilitated travel and trade. Concrete enabled them to build apartment buildings that were six floors high; previously buildings were restricted to two floors above ground level.

Everywhere in the ancient world, the Romans found processes and technologies that allowed them to make objects for mass use that previously had been superfluous luxuries only for aristocrats. There is no better illustration of this than Roman glass. The Romans learned how to blow glass, and that facilitated the dissemination of glass bottles, tumblers, jars, plates, and other objects throughout their world. Glass was made in huge blocks, some of them weighing as much as 20,000 pounds, in what is now Lebanon and Syria. These blocks were then sent to local workshops where they were broken up, and the glass was refired and blown into objects for everyday use.

TANGIBLE

Photo by Dr. Thomas Milton Kemnitz

REVIEW FOR CUMULATIVE QUIZ

com	together	**vita**	life	**intra**	within
vid	look	**cent**	one hundred	**pater**	father
ad	to	**matri**	mother	**fer**	carry
pop	people	**loco**	place	**sur**	over
alter	other	**contra**	against	**stell**	star
amat	love	**luna**	moon	**greg**	group
clam	cry out	**tang**	touch	**mar**	sea
junct	join	**luc**	light	**medi**	middle
tempor	time	**grat**	pleasing	**curr**	run
trans	across	**migr**	wander	**rupt**	break
clud	close	**se**	apart	**plu**	more
germ	vital	**fus**	pour	**culp**	blame
pugn	fight	**urb**	city	**numer**	number
acr	sharp	**per**	through	**anim**	mind
tort	twist	**sanct**	holy	**voc**	voice
punct	point	**trib**	pay	**cap**	take
pond	weight	**rect**	right		

placate	to appease	**commandeer**	officially take control
derision	ridicule	**intramural**	within an institution
vivacious	full of life	**centennial**	of a 100th anniversary
procure	to acquire	*ad infinitum*	again and again forever
retort	a quick, clever reply	**infer**	conclude from evidence
vitality	strength, energy	**audible**	able to be heard
videlicet (viz.)	namely	**benevolent**	charitable
paternal	of the father	**somber**	gloomy
matriarch	female head of family	**prostrate**	lying flat
populous	densely populated	**profuse**	abundant
localized	restricted to a place	**surfeit**	an excessive amount
altercation	a noisy argument	**contrary**	the opposite
stellar	of a star	**ostentatious**	showy
inexorable	inevitable	**indolent**	lazy
doleful	mournful	**alacrity**	eagerness
amatory	romantic	**sublunar**	under the moon
aggregate	a collected mass	**declaim**	speak against
entangled	snared, involved	**oblique**	indirect or slanting
pensive	thoughtful	**magnanimous**	generous
importune	to pester	**peremptory**	dictatorial

mariner	a sailor	**adjunct**	an unessential addition
elucidate	to explain	**mediate**	to intervene
temporize	to delay	**tacit**	unspoken
affable	friendly	**sanguine**	cheerfully confident
torpid	sluggish	**mortify**	profoundly humiliate
gratuitous	uncalled for	**concur**	to agree
transcend	to go beyond limits	**migratory**	moving seasonally
disruption	a disturbing interruption	**obsequious**	cringing, submissive
ignominy	disgrace	**acquiescence**	passive compliance
impassive	expressionless, without emotion	**impending**	about to happen
preclude	prevent	**seclude**	isolate from people
nonplussed	confused	**germane**	relevant
infusion	an inpouring	**verdure**	vegetation
equivocal	ambiguous	**orthodox**	traditional
profane	irreverent	**tumult**	disturbance
exculpate	to free from blame	**impugn**	to dispute the truth
urbane	refined	**enumerate**	to list
acrimony	bitterness	**incongruous**	incompatible
malevolence	ill will	**ambiguous**	uncertain
felicity	great happiness	**irrevocable**	unalterable
perspicacity	keen insight	**tortuous**	twisted
sanctimonious	self-righteous	**vociferate**	argue loudly
adjacent	adjoining	**transient**	existing briefly
latent	present but inactive	**livid**	bruised or pale
censure	strong criticism	**punctilious**	attentive to correct details
retribution	payback, punishment	**capitulate**	surrender
imponderable	difficult to answer	**rectify**	to make right, correct
epithet	a characterizing term	**abject**	miserable
eccentric	unconventional	**imperious**	overbearing
solicitude	concern		

352